# Crimson Sky

by Nikkele Shelton

ISBN: 978-0-692-39759-6
ISBN-13: 978-0-692-39759-6

# DEDICATION

To my "Mother Tibideaus"

Mary Stephens, Janet Smith, Bertha Armstrong, Clementine "Tina" Robinson, Carrie Jefferson, Peggy Bigelow, Dr. Aretha Coleman-Terry, Mary Williams, Annette "Sagacious" Barrett, Genevieve Moody-Cadwell, and Marian Hires Ellison (RIP).

# CONTENTS

# ACKNOWLEDGMENTS

I have too many people to thank for the completion of this fiction book, as the support has been overwhelming. However, I would be remiss if I did not specifically thank a few people who have been instrumental in this project. I would like to thank Jason Atkins for being a great friend and illustrator for *Crimson Sky*, my sister Raqueil for the final proofing, and Lemeicia Rambert for being the first to review the novel in its entirety. A very special note of gratitude goes to authors K.D. Smith (*Crystal Stairs*), Erica Kennedy (*The Tides that Bind*), my sister Dr. Augusta Massey, (*Lawyer Up! How to Be the 'Boss' at Your Own Firm*), and Professor Jeannie Cidel (*Schooling through Fruits and Vegetables*), whose invaluable advice helped me in the completion of this project. And last but not least, I must acknowledge my Father in Heaven who inspired me to share my thoughts with the world.

# 1 GENESIS

Sometimes I wished I was dead. Living life on the emotional edge was all I knew and I had no idea why. I came from a family of strong women who drank beer, smoked, played Spades, and kept loaded guns in every room. They lived hard and sometimes brought the street in the house. I saw things happen in the house that made me question my sanity because I had to walk a fine line between reality and the darkness of the intangible. All that came with that life was driven into my mind and parallel parked in my memory.

I often wished my life was like that of my best friend, Marigold, who was the epitome of normal with a mother, father, and stability. She had the kind of life that would never invite the thought of taking a bottle of pills and never waking up again. Mari didn't know what it was like to jump off a cliff in her mind, only to find she would never hit bottom because in real time she was sitting on her bed waiting for her nails to dry. My other best friend, Charisse, was the total opposite of Mari. I knew her longest—long enough to know that she could never accept me putting anyone before her. I can't say it was jealousy, but I can't say it was for a reason either.

"All I'm saying is when we get to college she is going to show her colors. Watch!" Charisse pronounced.

Charisse winced in preparation for a good slap because I could not stand to hear anyone talk about Mari and me not being friends. I had hoped her words were not that of a crazy person who had a moment of drunken clarity, but it was not the first time I'd heard them. My mother shared the same sentiments as well by telling me spirits that talk to her while asleep told her my friendships were headed for disaster. They also told her that something cataclysmic was going to happen to me during my senior year of college. Since that day my mother would often buy me jewelry with peridot, amethyst, and jade because each meant I would be protected from

1

something. Some bracelets even had an evil eye dangling from them like it had a detached retina. My mother would also never let anyone wash my hair and was funny about whose food I ate.

In her efforts to send me off to college protected and ready for anything, my last weekend home my mother threw a special party for me that escalated into a soiree for her friends that lasted all night. I invited Mari and Charisse, and as usual Mari didn't come. She wasn't allowed to come anywhere near my house. As far as they were concerned my family was not like their family and they had to protect their child from the influences they vigorously rejected. I still had a little hope that Mari would surprise me and magically appear, and that hope left fingerprints on the window so deep that Charisse had to pull me back into the party.

"Miss Bougie ain't coming!" Charisse yelled half drunk because under 21 was the legal drinking age in my house.

"You fit into this place more than I do!" I scolded.

I did my best to stay away from all the things my mother did because something inside of me would not let me have peace about imitating her ways. Despite those efforts, the bravado and keen ability to march to the beat of my own drummer leaked through my pores like sweat. My saving grace was that my aunt always said I had a little of my father in me. He was what a person would call "sensible". That small part of me stopped me from making the illogical and irrational my way of life. Unfortunately, I never formed a relationship with him because my mother made sure I never needed him. In her mind he was just passing through her life, but she did not think about him needing to pass through mine. We were Amazonian women as far as she was concerned.

As the night wore on, people began filing into the basement with clear instructions that the uninitiated had to remain upstairs. The uninitiated was me, Charisse, and a few people I grew up with from the block whose mothers and fathers were crazy, too. One of the teenaged crew, Roger, was anxious and wanted to see what they were doing in the basement.

"I bet they got an orgy going on!" he exclaimed, his eyes glistening and mouth dry from his over eagerness to see the forbidden. He had forgotten that my mother was one of the people in the basement who he claimed was part of his imaginary orgy, and he also forgot that I had a penchant for blanking out. I only remember swinging open the basement door and lifting my foot. Everyone else at the party remembered seeing my whole leg extended and Roger's back replacing my shoe. And as to confirm that it was a perfect fit, the tall, lanky, high yellow, big-mouthed kid landed at the bottom of the basement stairs positioned like a swastika. Then everyone heard someone say, "Put him on the table!" According to Charisse, the basement door then closed on its own.

After "Rogergate", the uninitiated supposedly heard him moaning

2

in pain and someone laughing as though wickedness was a joke. Someone else in the basement began talking in muted tones, like a deaf person trying to speak. Another friend from the block, Marie Colette, turned to me and looking white as a sheet shouted, "They're horsing!" She ran out of the house so fast that she didn't have time to tell her feet not to fail her.

I did not know what she meant by "horsing", but I heard enough to know it sounded like someone was possessed. With all the drinking and what not that was going on that night, in my mind *everyone* was possessed. Even though I had nothing but a mixed drink that even a baby could tolerate, I began to feel nauseated and threw up right at the basement door. And right on cue, my mother heard me and ran up the stairs, took off her white turban that she always wore when she had basement parties, sopped up my vomit, then headed back down below.

"I'll put that in the garbage," I offered before she disappeared into the darkness below.

"We need this."

I was too sick to protest and too sick to tend to my friends who were there on my behalf. All of them stood stock still as though they were afraid to leave and afraid to stay.

"Anyone want to follow Marie?" I offered. "Matter of fact, let's all go outside and get some air."

"What about Roger?" one of the crew asked.

"What about him?" I replied.

"But he's down there with them people. I mean, you know..."

"Roger is right where he wants to be, which is downstairs in grown folks' business. He..."

My speech was interrupted by a loud cry that made everyone's hair stand on the back of their necks, "Mamaaaaaaaan! Mamaaaaaaan! Ah! Ah! Ah!" The cries were accompanied by the sound of footfalls that were like hooves trampling on new earth.

"Y'all go outside," my mother commanded as she appeared at the top of the stairs. "And I mean right now!"

"Ma, what are you doing down there and why is Roger hollering like that?"

"Interrogation begins and ends with me. Now act like you heard what I said."

"I thought this was my party," I mumbled under my breath but loud enough for my mother to hear.

"I thought this was my house," my mother retorted lightning fast. "Checkmate."

I was agitated, embarrassed, and slightly confused. I was supposed to have a party to mark my going away to college, invited my friends who rarely came inside my house for reasons they probably felt were confirmed, and one was downstairs hollering for his mother like someone—or *something*—was jumping in and out of his body. My biggest fear was that someone would go to Roger's house and tell his mother something crazy, like he was being held hostage in my basement.

"Let's go in the backyard so we can see what's going on down there," I ordered. Everyone looked at each other as though we had to send someone as bait first. As though we were of one mind, everyone turned to Charisse who was still holding a beer in her hand.

"What y'all looking at me for?"

"You're the crash test dummy," said one.

"Toujours! Always!" said another.

"My backyard and my rules!" I declared.

"I think it would be your *mother's* backyard. Dang girl, checkmate twice in one night! Chess ain't your game," Charisse pointed out.

"I got your game, trust me. Keep it up. Get up over there and tell us what's going on with Roger."

"Alright," Charisse said while pointing her finger at me and slowly walking away. "But if something happens to me back there, I'ma get my gorillas on you."

"Fool, you ain't got no gorillas!"

Everyone busted out laughing because they knew it was an inside joke about my mother who used the phrase on anyone who got on her nerves. The first time I heard my mother use the term was when she went off on our neighbor to the right, an unmarried older man who lived with his ailing mother. Whenever my mother was out in the yard planting, he'd lean over the fence and try to talk to her. My mother was a rude person when she didn't feel like talking—and sometimes even when she did—so at times he would just be quiet and watch her while she pulled up weeds or planted vegetables. One day she got tired of him eyeballing her ampleness, slowly turned around, and fired all cylinders.

"I hope... I mean I swear before the Greek gods that you don't think you out here enticing somebody with that pot belly and peppercorn chest hair. I really don't!"

"Miss Esther, no harm intended. I just like to be outside when you're outside, that's all. I like a little conversation."

"Oh you want more than conversation!" my mother accused. "I don't want nothing you got. Don't want it today, don't want it tomorrow, and I sure don't want it after death. No indeed!"

"Beg pardon, Esther?"

"If you don't get that hamburger meat outta my line of sight, I'm gonna get my gorillas on you. You old deaf bandicoot! You got some nerve with that gut trailing the ground making a path in the grass! I declare, I think this is the first time I seen a cart going before the horse! And my daughter is out here too? Jeepers Creepers!"

"Miss Esther! Now it don't take all that sass."

"You like it," my mother said matter-of-factly as she turned her back to resume what she was doing. "Now let me feel your eyes on me again."

Mr. Bandicoot went back into the house with his gut between his legs, but not before giving me a puzzled look. I am pretty sure I looked at him in puzzlement as well, but I don't remember if I was amazed by the peppercorn, the trail he left in the grass, or that he seemed happy my mother spoke to him despite the green slime that covered every word that shot out of her mouth. I guess he *did* like it.

Charisse made her way to the side of the backyard that bordered Bandicoot's house and we all stood at a safe distance in case something happened. We could see Charisse crouching down by the basement window and carefully placing her beer a couple of feet from her. The rest were cracking jokes to scare her saying, "The dog is loose!" and "There's somebody behind you!" Charisse waved her hand to tell us to quiet down. She peered into the window with squinted eyes due to the dim light it offered. Then all of a sudden, she put her hand over her mouth. *I hope this fool doesn't scream!* Her eyes grew wider, she wrinkled up her nose, then cocked her neck back like something was about to come out of the chamber.

"Oh shoot oh shoot oh shoot!" my friend Creepy exclaimed. I called him that because he always walked around at night by himself with no destination in mind, which I found creepy.

"What are you saying that for? You're not even over there," I reprimanded, which made him turn around and parler francais. "Y'all stop talking that booja boo and pay attention!" I whispered.

I was losing my patience between everyone murmuring and Charisse making faces, yet not signaling us that it was okay to come over. We were so busy being frustrated that we did not notice Charisse come charging towards us like a bull, and we all became stooges running and shoving each other as though we didn't know which way to go. I turned around to see where Charisse was and it was like slow motion the way it happened. In her drunken stupor and fear of whatever she saw, her left foot snagged a flower pot. As she began her descent to the ground, she waved her arms in slow motion as though she were trying to flag down a taxi on the moon. Everyone just stopped and stared, eyes widening and heads oscillating one centimeter per second. Creepy so happened to be in Charisse's path and instead of catching her, he crossed his arms and stepped back. Right before she hit the grass, Charisse turned to Creepy and mouthed something to him. He thought she was insulting him because he did not catch her, but as she lay on the ground she pointed to something behind him. He had accidentally knocked over her beer. We all laughed so hard that we temporarily forgot about our mission. I was holding my sides, Creepy was quiet, and the others were running in circles laughing hysterically.

"Did you see anything?" I asked in between laughs.

"Yea, I saw something."

"What?" Creepy asked.

"He was lying on the table and somebody was writing on his back. They put this green paste on his forehead…"

"They did the sign of the cross?" one asked.

"A little "t". That's all I know."

"That's it, yea. Go on."

"Then it looked like somebody drank something from a bottle and walked around the room spitting in everyone's face!"

"Charisse, come on now," I said in disbelief. "My mother is not going to have somebody in her basement spitting in people's faces."

"That's what they do!" someone yelled from behind, freezing us all in fear. The whole of us turned our heads slowly as though we had rust in our joints or were churning butter with a splintered wooden spoon. It was Marie Colette, who had come back with Roger's mother.

"Where your people from?" Roger's mother asked me in her thick, muted, French- sounding accent with a touch of island.

"New York," I said, fearful that she would do something that would cause my mother to emerge from the ground with a cold piece of steel.

"But where else? How you from New York and your mother throw *parties?*"

I looked at her like the crazy she was. Who *doesn't* throw parties?

"You don't know what they do down there? You don't know what kind of party I'm talking about, do you?" she asked. Her shock to my oblivion about whatever it was she thought I should know was apparent. "Where your people *really* from? Tell me. *Maintentant!*"

"My grandmother was from Louisiana but the rest of us were born up here."

"Ah, I see now. It has not passed down to you yet. That's strange. You should have been inducted by now. Anyway, no more talking about this. I came for my son and I want him out here now or I will summon all of heaven! Let me in your house!"

Marie Colette could see my frustration over Roger's mother talking in code and confusing me more than I was already, but I decided to ask her to wait outside while I went in to see what Roger was doing. In the meantime, Charisse knew to run interference by going on and on about how we kept telling Roger not to go downstairs with the grownups who were playing cards, drinking, and dancing with the night.

I eventually returned with Roger, who looked like his feathers were ruffled, and he had some wet spots on his face and shirt like a can of soda exploded on him. He had some green stuff on his forehead that his mother wiped away with a soft cloth doused in some spicy smelling oil.

"Nan non Papa a, Pitit la, ak Sentespri a... amen," she said, after which she made what they call the sign of the cross.

"They're Catholic," Creepy whispered loud enough for the Pope to hear all the way at the Vatican. "She said in the name of the Father, the Son, and the Holy Spirit."

"Thanks interpreter," I retorted.

No sooner than I thanked Creepy for his information interjection, my mother appeared at the front door. Roger's mother's vocal chords wanted a piece of the action and erupted into a song of rebuke, "Satan, Seyè a regle ou! The Lord rebuke you! Go back to Hell you demon! Ale kounye a!"

My mother began shouting in return, cursing the catholic god and tapping a crooked staff on the railing of the front steps as though she were summoning something from beneath the house.

"Invader!" my mother accused. "Invader! Your rebukes against me will fall to the ground and die!"

Everyone stood stock still as the two women battled it out with words—some in English, some in French, and some in Kreyol—taking turns rebuking the other and calling on whomever they relied on to help them fight against the opposing force. Roger's mother made a quick motion towards a set of cement gray statues that looked like angels with huge wings, which my mother claimed she kept as a means to keep people with opposing spirits from putting curses on the house. Roger's mother hurled the remainder of the spicy oil she poured on Roger at the statues. The final drop seemed to generate a bolt of lightning that struck the lawn with so much alacrity that we missed the light and only heard the sound. The victim was my mother's largest statue, the one she called The Guardian. It had split in half while the smaller ones fell backward. At the sight, my mother ran into the house to get reinforcements while Roger and his mother took the opportunity to get out of dodge. As mother and son walked away, Marie Colette ran back to tell me something.

"Your mother is a witch," she accused. "I bet they took Roger's blood. He look like he got a demon now."

"What did you tell her?" I demanded.

"I lied. If she knew they took him, she would be back here with the Pope and the ghosts of Toussaint L'Overture and Dessaline, both! And I bet you he threw up, too. I bet you! *Certainement!*"

I remained silent and just watched her until the moon's admiration of her silhouette vanished. I did not want to give credence to anything she said, and if she wanted to believe that the stuff my mother did down below was real, let her. However, I could not explain away the incident that occurred that night. Despite what my eyes told me, my logical mind convinced me that lightning did strike, or the statue was on the verge of breaking anyway and one hard footstep on the lawn was all it took to give way. Or maybe Mr. Bandicoot was in the yard walking about and the boom was his much despised belly hitting the ground. And as expected, my friends were not convinced and decided they needed to leave before they too would fall in the way of some special oil and split in half. One by one everyone began to file out. Charisse was drunk and remained while Creepy was getting anxious.

"Time for your nighttime creep?" I asked.

"I'm compelled to shake hands with the night. Don't follow me."

"You don't have to worry about that. No, nuh uh! Have at it and don't save any for me. Gooooood night!"

"Got it. Good night my baby," Creepy said as he leaned over and kissed my cheek as close as he could get to my mouth without signaling my reflexes. Even though we were just friends I liked his innocent kisses. They were sweet like a brother's love.

Charisse gave Creepy a look as though she were waiting for him to say goodbye to her in a special way, but in his mind he was leaning back again to give her space to fall. To Charisse there was no such thing as a man being in our presence and not paying her attention.

"That's why you ain't got no girl and the only one you seem to like ain't thinking about you!" Charisse snarled.

As Creepy walked away, I thought I saw him lean back again. He looked at me and winked. It was as though he knew some day Charisse would fall and fall and fall and not get back up again. I knew it too.

I went back into the house to find my mother standing in the basement doorway with her arms crossed and tapping her foot to a song that never made it to radio. She wore a clean turban and puffed away at a dirty cigarette in her right hand.

"I don't know who the hell that lady think she is coming up in my yard like she gonna make somebody give somebody up. She know better."

My mother continued to rant about Roger's mother's trespasses until someone from the basement called her back downstairs. She gave me a once- over before she turned around.

"What was that for?" I queried. "What did I do?"

"Where your friend at? Tell her there's more in the house."

I bolted out the door because I forgot Charisse was still outside drunk and probably was on her hands and knees trying to sop up her spill. Instead, she was standing on the sidewalk watching Creepy walk down the

8

street.

"Let's follow him," she suggested. "We ain't doing nothing anyway."

"How about I walk you to your house because you are unfit for company right now, talking crazy."

"But I was fit to look through the window and risk getting zombied while all y'all played lookout from 100 feet away."

I couldn't argue against that fact and she couldn't argue against me walking her home, so we began our journey on foot to the other side of town. I was never afraid to walk around at night because I carried concealed weapons everywhere I went; it was something I learned from my mother. I was to always be prepared for anything and hand to hand combat didn't always cut it. If I didn't have a weapon, I must always scan the area to see if I could make one if I had to.

"You can wear a skirt all you want, but you better have something up under there if someone comes at you wrong. Trust your mama on this one," my mother said one night while Aunt Reesie was over.

"Did Reesie ever tell you what happened to one of her friends over at the park one night?" my mother asked.

"Don't scare the girl, Esther," Reesie pleaded. But my mother's eyes communicated that the story must be told and Reesie obliged. "Well, this dumb girl wasn't from around here and she was trying to make her way to Wayne's house wearing a cheap yellow dress and party shoes."

"You mean Wayne the numbers runner?" I asked.

"Yea, that Wayne," my mother interrupted. "He owes me for last week, by the way."

"Esther, I'm telling the girl a story and you all in yourself. So where was I? Oh yea, so she on foot, right, with those cheap clothes on and call herself taking a shortcut through the park just because the lights were on, but she had someone following her and..."

"BLAP! She caught herself a knock!"

"Esther! Who telling this story?"

"Apparently somebody who talks at a slow pace with an affinity for too much detail! Suzi, the lady was raped under the lights in the park. People heard her screaming and carrying on and even saw the man, but nobody did nothing. She ran all the way to *this* house. Past Wayne's house, mind you, and ran to *this* house looking for protection."

With Reesie looking cross because my mother snatched the bone from her mouth, my mother continued to share how she, Reesie, and my mother's friend, Gina, packed up in the car with aluminum bats and firearms looking for the guy. They eventually found him sitting in the picnic area away from the bright lights where he raped Reesie's friend.

"So what happened?" I asked rhetorically.

"One good turn deserved another. When we got done with him he had a bad case of the "ain't got no" !" my mother proudly confessed. "He ain't got no teeth, he ain't go no crown jewels, he ain't got no working left eye, and he sure ain't got no woman because of all the other ain't gots. And he ain't got no money because I made him pay me to spare his life."

Whenever my mother shared those types of stories, she would go into a long sermon about how a woman is to carry herself and to never let anyone take advantage of her. Even though she surrounded herself with various men, she didn't trust them.

"Now listen to what I say. No man, I don't care who he is, will ever violate a woman on my watch. No man! So you hear me good, Young Suzi. Don't you ever, ever, ever let no man put his hands on you. I don't care if he brushes up against you in a crowded subway. You take him to task, you hear me?"

Reesie rolled her eyes as my mother railed against men and how vile they could be— dangerous even—and that no matter how good he is to a woman, she must be ready to pull the trigger or swing the bat at any moment. Reesie had a different perspective about men because she was not as independent as my mother; she was more of a kept woman. My aunt was so kept that she never had to have her own place because whomever she dated either moved her in right away or would have a separate house where she could live until the relationship fizzled out.

I replayed that conversation in my mind as Charisse and I walked into the darkness in order for me to get her home safely. I could have easily called a cab, but I wanted to take a walk in the night air and hang out a little. Like Creepy, I was a night person. But unlike Creepy, I always had a destination in mind. I wasn't too worried about what could happen because my neighborhood was small and there weren't too many people that separated one from knowing the other. Rarely would I encounter a person I never saw before. If I did, I knew to put my hand up under my skirt.

Despite the weirdness of the night before, I woke up somewhat rested and began the day as usual going to the store to run errands. I returned with a bag of goodies in hand, including my mother's numbers that she played religiously. Like clockwork, I passed Creepy as he was just ending his night walk. No one ever knew where he went or where he was going when he returned because sometimes he would just pass his house like he was walking on an endless highway. It never stopped us from exchanging pleasantries.

"Creepy."

"You."

I wanted to take a stroll down familiar places to record all I would leave behind when I traveled South for college. I anticipated something great would happen to me, while my mother had a sense of foreboding. I had high hopes for something new to enter my life and had no expectation of things going other than the way I wanted. The boogeyman can say what he wanted to say; that was my mother's belief, not mine. But even though it was just hocus pocus to me, I did not like the idea of our household being run by figments of my mother's alcohol and "earth cigarette" induced fantasies of something bigger than herself hiding under her bed while waiting to whisper sweet omens in her ear.

"Do you hear that?" my mother asked me one time when there was a thunderstorm out.

"Thunder?" I answered with a tinge of sarcasm.

"The big man is walking up and down the block. Somebody put the evil eye on this house and he is finding out who it is."

I ignored my mother as she continued to talk about the mysterious big man whose voice sounded like thunder and tears showered like rain.

"Watch! When the rain is done and I see the sun, I will find the one. Now puff it or give it."

I gave as I handed my mother her special smoke for an eye condition she didn't have. For some reason I always wanted to hold it for her, maybe secretly hoping I would muster up the nerve to try it if it got close enough to my mouth. The reality was I really liked the smell of it and I liked to watch the smoke as it curled its way around the air I breathed. I would pretend the smoke was my thoughts weaving in and out of the minds of whoever would happen to be there at the time. They didn't know I was secretly making them think what I wanted. I would think things like *Go home* and *Eat at your own house*, but most times it would just be my mother and me sitting at the table bonding over her crazy stories, and me holding her herbal delight in my efforts to feel occupied. My mother proceeded to congratulate herself that her child did not imitate all of her ways.

"You know I'm sad you're leaving. I don't know what I'm going to do with you gone. Who is going to listen to my stories? Who is going to hold my piece of sweet paper in between puffs? Who am I going to cook for and tell to tie up her hair at night?"

I knew that part of our conversation was just a soliloquy. I had no response for what my mother said. No doubt she would miss me, but her life was separate from mine even though we lived in the same house. At times I felt like I was just there, even though I knew my mother loved me and would never let anything happen to me. For whatever reason I had no feelings I wanted to share. My life was strange and I knew it. The only way I could cope with that strangeness was to create a world outside of my home with Charisse and Mari.

"Now I'm going to give you some rules to follow while you're away," my mother began. I knew the speech was coming about what company to keep, trust no man, and never beg, borrow, or steal.

"First, watch the company you keep," my mother said between drags. "Hold this while I talk. I intend to point my finger."

My mother often pointed her middle finger at me in place of her pointer because that was what she believed the world did to us every day and she wanted me to remember that.

"Now I know when it came to your friends you never listened to me, but believe me, I kept an eye on them in my own way. But when you get to college you got to protect your reputation. People judge you by the birds you flock with. Naw, wait. The birds *with whom* you flock, College Girl. Ha!"

I knew she was talking about Charisse, the one who was a loosey goosey and didn't care about her own reputation.

"Your friend Charisse, how do I say it? Out of respect for you and so you don't get mad and crumble my smoke between your fingers, I will just say she ain't too fresh down there. How about that? Everybody here know it and when you get to that campus everybody there gonna know it too."

"So?" I said. "It's not me."

"Makes no difference. People don't care if it's you or not. They just care that they got a story to tell. Mark my words! You get away scot free here because everybody knows you and they are acutely aware of my wrath. But in college nobody knows you. You just another one stepping off the bus. And second, don't trust no man. Men lie and they ain't no good. Point period blank. And last, don't ever, never, never beg, borrow, or steal. If you beg, people look down on you. If you borrow, people feel they got something over you. If you steal, you just plain sorry. Now pass it back to me."

My mother realized there was nothing to pass back because she had gone on so long about other things that it burned down to a roach that was way too small for tweezers. I had a stunned look on my face as my mother began to talk again, but she switched gears and started talking about religion.

"For the most part I left you alone to think what you want to think as long as you wasn't trying to be no christian. I don't care what you do, don't do that! They talk devil this and devil that, and they got more devil than Satan got horns."

The only organized religion my mother talked about was christianity and how she hated it. She had such a disdain for christians that on christmas she would say "Happy Halloween!" for spite. When someone sneezed she would say, "May the evil eye protect you!" For whatever reason, I knew her disdain for christians had less to do about the religion and more about a christian who was the object of her fury. However, I chose to believe in nothing with the possibility of something; it just wasn't deep enough for me to will the answer into my space. But somehow life had a way of spiting my will.

To get some fresh air, and away from my mother going on and on about things I've heard before, I decided to go outside, throw my head back, and yell at whomever was in the night sky, "Let me breathe! You're suffocating me!"

No one replied back except a silent, blood red moon that seemed to jump out of my head and into the sky. It was hovering over the neighborhood and had its own special effect on anyone who would dare look up. It cast a crimson shadow that bled over my face. My mother came to the window to see what the commotion was.

"So you a wolf now? Get in this house!"

The moon jumped back inside my head as I entered the house and it made a point to remind me that it was not made of cheese. Rather, it was hard with craters and not too many people visited there. It was bright enough for all to see and looked close enough to touch, but the reality was it was far away in its own lonely world waiting to hear another story from its mother while she smoked the tails of comets.

My last weekend home was filled with a mixture of joyful anticipation and a little anxiety. I was ready to venture out and have a whole new experience, but at the same time I had to find myself in new territory filled with strange faces and paradigms. Thankfully, I would have my two best friends at my side who also were accepted into the same school.

At home I had my mother's reputation to protect me from having people invade my space. My boldness came from knowing people would back down because they didn't want to deal with the repercussions of messing with Esther's daughter. Besides, my mother curried the favor of every person in the neighborhood with a prison record. All she had to do was make a phone call and whomever she had a problem with would have to RSVP to the nearest hospital. But I was going to college hundreds of miles away and there was nothing my mother could do except make threats.

It wasn't even my idea to go to school so far away. I had applied to only local schools so that I'd be a stone's throw away from my own bedroom if I ever wanted to come home. One day Mari's mother asked me to which schools I applied and when I told her, she made sure Mari applied to none of them and also forbade her to tell me where she had been accepted. Being the consummate detective, I went to Mari's guidance counselor and made a passing comment that I wondered if I could get into the schools where Mari applied. The counselor gave an emphatic affirmation and went so far as to say she had hoped I would apply to Mari's first choice school because she thought it was more suited to my major in engineering. So I applied, got in on an early decision, and surprised Mari with the news. Once Charisse found out, she applied as well.

My intention was to fly down South and have my items shipped, but my mother was superstitious about the whole thing. I overheard her talking to her friend Rita about it a few weeks before I left.

"She ever been down there before?" Rita asked.

"No."

"You?"

"Nah. Well not in person."

"Esther, I told you about flying at night without me watching your body. You're not there yet. You're not your momma."

"Between you and my sister telling me I ain't my momma! I got the gift. I got all the gifts! I can make you and everybody I know disappear!"

"Calm down, Es. Calm down. You already know I will come to you, sit on the edge of your bed, and paralyze you. Matter of fact, I did it before. You thought it was your..."

"That was you? That was you riding my back?" my mother said in disbelief as she leaned back in her chair to get a better look at Rita before the green slime shot out of her mouth.

"I have to watch you, Esther. I have to watch you sometimes. You go ahead of the group and they don't like that. You pay too much reverence to your mother's spirit. The spirits say you have to let her go."

"Let's get back to my daughter. She is leaving me and I need to keep watch."

"This is what we can do."

Rita proceeded to tell her that I could not fly but needed to drive so that I could leave footprints from door to door. That way when my mother sent a spirit to watch over me, it would know the way. I thought the whole thing was comical because there was no way anybody could watch me who wasn't there, and nobody could fly around at night and visit people in bed and paralyze them. Science already proved that the brain secreted a chemical while a person sleeps to keep the body from moving around too much. Sometimes a person may wake up before the chemical stopped secreting and find herself unable to move. My mother always termed it as a "witch riding on your back" or my grandmother trying to tell her something from the grave.

"Well won't it be the same if she flies?" my mother asked.

"No. You don't want to send an air spirit. Send a land spirit. The air spirit will have too much to contend with. Remember, she's going to the Bible Belt. They pay attention to the principalities and powers in the air, but not so much to the ones down below.

"Why?"

"Because they look like them. In some of those places you can't tell a demon from a saint."

"A saint? How about an *ain't*?! That's what I call 'em! Them holiness christians," my mother muttered. "Them holiness ones in church all day every day and talking about rivers of living water coming out their mouths! I hate 'em!"

The more I listened, the more I was ready to leave home. I was ready to see what life was like without hearing ghost stories at night and the stress of hoping one day my mother would wake up, get a job, and mingle with normal people in order to vacate her private world. As far as I was concerned, the lease had expired a long time ago.

I spent most of the day making sure I packed all that I needed. I had a mind to pack my best clothes and shoes, but my mother said I needed to feel people out first before I sprung my wardrobe on them. My clothes were not flashy, but they were expensive. My mother's wardrobe mainly consisted of a pink bathrobe, fuzzy slippers, and a cigarette, but she had some fine threads tucked away for the times she would actually leave the house. The men she dated would often buy her clothes, sometimes in a size too small, and she would pass them to me. Other times she would call my aunt, who used to be a buyer for a major retail store, and have her take me to boutiques or help me order from catalogues. My mother had a thing about me wearing anything somebody next door could have bought. My mother would always say, "Your clothes got to make a statement. They got to say *me*, not *me too*."

When I grew tired of being paranoid about what I would possibly leave behind, I decided to walk to Charisse's house. I could not stand the ground her father walked on, neither did I fancy her siblings, but I walked in the house like I owned it because I kind of did. My mother had more than one run in with Charisse's father, which gave me carte blanche whenever I walked up in the yard. I would always see her father under the hood of a car and he would always look up at me, grunt, and yell for Charisse.

Charisse, being the bull in the china shop she was, would always come charging out of the door like she was a Jack-in-the-Box. She had an old school screen door that was mostly metal, and the sound it made as she banged her way into the great outdoors was the most annoying thing I ever heard. It was to the point where whenever I saw Charisse coming, I would hear the door in my mind, "Bang!" And strangely enough, sometimes I would hear that noise every blue moon, and coincidentally those would be the times Charisse would wind up at my house seeking refuge from the crazy in hers.

Charisse always wore the same outfit but in different colors; pink bubblegum stretch jeans, a white button down top, and a red jacket that was the mate to a pair of jogging pants. Other days it would be white, black, blue, or pale yellow bubblegums with a white button down shirt and that same track jacket. I hated the way she dressed, but what she wore became more like her uniform. If she didn't wear those items, she would not be Charisse. And the top it all off, she always wore the same high top Reeboks that women wore when they did aerobics.

There were times when I really did believe Charisse was stupid, but she would always have these superior moments when she made more sense than anyone. The wisdom just came out of her mouth like a diamond blown out of darkest part of the human anatomy. But those moments were random, which imitated her life. She never seemed to be one for direction, yet her life seemed to stay on course enough for her to achieve all of the essentials other people our age did.

"Girl, I am so ready to get out of here! I can't wait! You know I heard them boys Down South are fine!" Charisse said. "They got that country accent and lick their lips and put their hands to their chins when they talk and..."

*And shut up, Charisse.*

"And they lean back too," I added, deliberately sounding aloof so that she would change the subject.

"Yea, like they want to take a good look at you. Yea. When they take a look at me..."

"Not in those jeans," I interrupted. "Matter of fact, what are you taking to school?"

Charisse failed to realize that she could not bring her bubblegum style to a college campus. I knew the only way she would go off to college with a better wardrobe was if I helped her get one. At the time I wasn't sure if I should tell her what I thought because she was very sensitive and would look for a reason to play the victim. After some thought, I realized it didn't matter. She was my friend and I wanted her to represent herself a little better.

"Charisse, you got some new clothes to bring with you?" I asked in a careful tone, which was not my usual M O.

"My jeans and white shirts. I asked my father for some money, but he said I don't need no new clothes to learn."

"Oh. Are you all packed?"

"Yea."

I asked her to take me into the house so I could make sure she had all that she needed. Since I was a master packer, I would help her decide what she should take on the first trip and what she could get when the seasons changed.

When we walked into the house, I felt Charisse's father's eyes burn a hole in my head as I followed his daughter inside. He looked like a snake to me with his small, beady eyes and slick, hairless head. I could easily blame it on my mother for why he didn't like me as much as I didn't like him, but something in his eyes made me feel there was more to it than that. It was as if he did not want anyone around who was not kin to him; like a new thought or way of doing things would corrupt the cult he formed in his home. But, he had to acquiesce and let me stroll in and out before my mother would make an appearance and remind him he needed to stay under the hood of his car or she would burn his eyes out with two sticks and toast them like marshmallows. The thought of my mother having told him that made me let out a loud chuckle, and as odds would have it, I so happened to make eye contact with the object of my private ridicule. I relished in the moment as I turned my head and let the door bang behind me.

"You old black dog! I will burn your eyes out with two sticks and roast them bad boys like marshmallows!" my mother screamed into the phone. Charisse's father took money from a woman my mother knew and didn't pay her back. The woman came to our house and asked my mother to put a spell on him so that she would get her money back.

"Did you lie in bed with him?" my mother asked.

"Why, what…"

"Shut it down. You did. I can tell by the look on your lips. So in light of that, I can't put no spell on him."

"Why not? I got money!" the lady assured her.

"If you *had* money you wouldn't be over here trying to *get* money. One of us is making sense here, the other is not. You got me? Plus, if you shared his bed you will share his misfortune. Your souls are still tied together because you have not let him go."

What my mother opted was to do things without all the chicken bones and digging a ditch to bury a dollar bill with his name on it. Instead, she decided to use good old-fashioned threats. The conversation ended with Charisse's father sending his oldest son, Fairisaac, with half the money and a promise for the other half.

"Who names their son a name like that and still got bad credit? That's some bad luck right there. Real bad!" my mother declared. "And as for you, my lady friend, don't come over here asking for no spell when your business ain't finished." My mother knew that as soon as the second half of the payment came in, the woman would be right back over to Charisse's house hollering like a cat on a fence in the name of love.

"Nasty! I shudder at the thought," my mother said as she ushered the woman out of the house.

I was never one to be too judgmental about what people could or could not afford, but Charisse's house felt like an above ground dungeon to me. The kitchen smelled like "cooking". If you walked in her kitchen with your eyes closed, you would automatically know there were jars of chicken and fish grease, and a heavy, black, post-emancipation period frying pan on the stove with week-old bacon grease that had solidified ten times over. You would also know that there was a white toaster in the corner that had burnt corners, a microwave with sauce splashed on its ceiling, and a refrigerator with red Kool Aid stains on the handle. There was a small, portable, black and white TV on the counter that lost its knobs, so there had to be a small pair of pliers nearby to change the channel. There was also a little ball of foil rolling around, no doubt to plug up the hole in the broken antenna in case the reception ever got bad. I knew it was Charisse who broke it because she liked to play with things that collapsed, and sometimes she would pull the thing up just a little too hard and...*bang*. I wanted to believe that the kitchen had seen better days, but like everything and everyone in the house, it had been used and abused.

"Charisse, now I know better than that!" I exclaimed when I saw she had her clothes packed in old and dirty duffle bags. I was about to say more when I saw Charisse's eyes well up. I excused myself to use her phone, made a call to my aunt Reesie, and came back to Charisse's bedroom with a smile on my face.

"We are going shopping, girl. Reesie is going to pick us up and get us whatever we need."

Instead of saying thank you, Charisse protested.

"I can't bring that stuff back here! My father would kill me!"

"We will take them to my house and pack there. Don't worry about it. Charisse?"

"What?"

"Why didn't you say anything?"

She threw herself on her bed and started a weeping and a wailing. I knew without her having to say so that she was scared. She never had much, and what she did have she pretended to love so as to not feel the weight of the prosperity of the other people around her. It made me feel bad for opening my mouth about the duffle bags. There were times I could be insensitive, but I really didn't mean to.

Before I had a chance to have my own pity party over my verbal faux pas, I heard a horn blow outside.

"That's Reesie. We had better go or we will have to pull a stunt move and jump in the car while it's moving!"

Reesie was also not a fan of Charisse's father. She never had nasty altercations with him, but whenever they would see each other in the road my aunt would always say something slick to make him feel uncomfortable. True to form, Reesie already had the doors open while anticipating us jumping in with alacrity. As I stunt doubled my way into the front seat, she leaned over me, her gold chains dangled forward to give her cleavage room to breathe, and she stuck her head close to the window to recite a few parting words.

"You old grizzled, nasty, dirty, stanky fool!"

Before Charisse's father had a chance to slither his head around the hood to see who was yelling at him, my aunt pulled off with the screech of drag racer.

"Reesie, why did you do that?"

"Because he's uh old grizzled, nasty, dirty, stanky fool. Oh, excuse me...hi Charisse!"

Charisse gave a small "Hi Reesie" and zipped her track jacket up to her nose, put her hands inside her sleeves, and crossed her arms. She was checking out.

"Charisse, we gonna shop 'til we drop, hear? We gonna get you some tops and bottoms, draws, bras, lotion, all that stuff. And I got some luggage for you, too. We care about you, honey. We love you in this family. You a little crazy and off-kilter sometimes, but that's another story. With a daddy like that..."

"Reesie," I sang in the key of C so that she'd realize she was going off on a tangent.

"We want you to have the best," she continued. "You can't be representing our town looking like no ragamuffin. I'm done."

Despite my aunt's awkward way of letting Charisse know we cared, Charisse gave the back of my seat a soft kick. That was her way of letting me know she knew how my aunt was and that therefore she was not going to take offense. Not one to miss a beat, my aunt blurted out on cue, "Don't be back there talking about me with your feet!"

We all laughed out loud and knew we were going to have a good time exchanging Charisse's old baggage for new. In my heart, I had hoped us venturing to new territory would mean the same.

We were in the throes of a successful day of shopping that turned Charisse into a whole other person. Knowing she would begin a new school with a fashionable upper-hand was appealing to her. There was no doubt the wheels of lust were spinning in her head as she selected the most fitted and curve hugging clothes. However, there was no way she could say she shopped with Reesie and not pick clothes that would look good on her, so she found half of the things she chose had to be put back.

Charisse was in awe of my aunt as we went from store to store and saw her produce neither paper nor plastic. Reesie only shopped where people knew her and the man who kept her. All she had to do was say his name and the store would bill him for it. But Charisse's awe quickly turned into bewilderment as she saw my aunt arguing back and forth with the lady at the counter.

"I'm sorry but you can't shop here without your own form of payment," the clerk said.

I had no problems leaving the store empty-handed because we did well in the previous stores we'd shopped, but the clerk's words made Reesie draw back and put her hands on her hips, looking around the store for words she never carefully chose. She was able to find two or three from way back in the fitting room, and one or two more from behind the counter. She even pulled one out of my head and promised to return it. By the time Reesie was done, she had randomly called forth words from every corner of the store until the clerk was standing at the register looking as though she was baptized in acid.

"Miss, I am going to have to call the police."

"Call 'em! Call 'em! You trick! Do you know who I am? Do you know who I am? You just try it!"

"I know who you are! That's why I can't let you charge those clothes to my husband's account!"

Charisse and I both heard a needle scratch on a record, a car stop on a dime, and a chicken grabbed by the neck so hard that it barely had time to cluck. With feathers and words flying everywhere, we stopped what we were doing and snuck out of the store like two robbers surprised by the sound of the owner's car in the driveway. We left Reesie standing at the counter arguing with the longsuffering wife who probably knew about her for a long time, and who finally mustered up the nerve to confront her. No doubt she probably heard my aunt was making rounds at the shops and zipped over to stand behind the counter to pretend to be the clerk.

"So how did shopping go?" my mother asked upon our return with a half amused look on her face. I didn't answer because I knew she already knew what happened. My mother had eyes and ears in the street, and she always got the news first.

Charisse and I went upstairs to admire our spoils. Reesie decided against Charisse taking her clothes home but rather ordered her to pack them at my house so that her father would have nothing to say. It was also so that Charisse's half-siblings wouldn't get jealous and go through her clothes. That was probably why she didn't have much because everyone in the house was a dog for other people's items.

"She act like a princess, just like her tore up dead mama," Charisse's half-sibling, Tasha, said one day as her other siblings in the room, Fairisaac and Trina, watched the action with smirks on their faces. "You don't need no new clothes to go to no 9th grade."

"Word! For real do'! You don't keep them on anyway, ho!" Fairisaac chimed in with way too much conviction.

Charisse backed herself into a corner as her half siblings continued to threaten to divide the spoils of her new school clothes. Her deceased mother's only child, Charisse always had to fight for a space in the home her mother bought for Charisse's no good, junkyard daddy and even junkier kids by two previous marriages. Charisse assumed the usual position of balling herself up and rocking back and forth with her ears covered.

"There she go again rocking. That's why she the way she is. She crazy," Tasha continued.

"Yup," Trina added. "You smell like you been in the boys

bathroom doing stuff. Yup."

"Yea, you take them t-shirts, Isaac," Tasha commanded. "And I think I'll have me a yellow shirt, some jeans, some of this, some of that. Trina, take the whole bag. Teach her a lesson."

"Daddy!" Charisse yelled. "Daddy!"

Charisse's father appeared out of nowhere as though he was already close by to supervise his youngest daughter get bullied.

"Ain't nothing going on in here, Charisse. Stop hollering," he said.

"They trying to take my clothes!" Charisse accused. "My new clothes for school."

"You can't share with your sisters and brother? Stingy! Just like your mama. Stingy! I bet she in the grave rationing the dirt. Humph!"

Everyone laughed as Charisse continued to sit in a ball in the corner and slice her wrists with an imaginary knife. She wished she was dead—if at least for a moment. That was the last time Charisse bought new clothes for school and the start of her uniform that she wore the day we went shopping.

We talked into the night discussing what we would wear our first day of class. It was the conversation she always wanted to have in high school but couldn't. I knew it would make Charisse feel better if I joined in her excitement. It was important to her to belong and feel special, even though most times she acted as though she didn't have a care in the world. That was her armor—the dingy behavior that protected her from revealing the abused little girl trapped inside a track jacket and bubblegum jeans. Charisse never said it, but I could always tell she was severely neglected because the decibels of her voice always had the sound of the lack of attention. Despite our closeness, she never fully revealed all that went on in her home. I always had to fill in the blanks whenever she ran to my house for cover. I offered to let her spend the night so that she could pack, eat, and just hang out on our last Saturday at home.

As the night wore on, my mother's friends zipped in and out of the house for various things. During the day we had a closed door policy, but at night my mother always had someone stopping by to go down to the basement and whisper in her ear. Our house was large enough so that I could go upstairs and not be disturbed, but Charisse was the one who brought the disturbance that night. On her way to the bathroom she crossed paths with my mother's friend, Federline. He was black as night with flaring nostrils, and wore an arm full of bracelets made of copper with shells and colored beads. He reminded me of the witch doctors I'd seen on TV, except he was clean shaven and didn't wear traditional clothes.

"Who is that one?" he said to my mother as he saw Charisse slide through the hall to the bathroom. His accent was heavy and words certain. He spoke as though people called him Mufasa.

"Charisse, Suzi's raggedy friend."

"She wears a red dress."

"That ain't no red…oh."

"Yes, yes, Madame. You see what I mean? Don't look at her. Look *through* her."

"Uh huh. So what you saying? I already know she's been touched, and not by no angel," my mother said matter-of-factly.

"Dress red as blood," Federline said as if my mother said nothing. "Red as blood. When she comes back, look at her again."

My mother waited for Charisse to return from the bathroom so that she could see what Federline was talking about. When she came out, my mother gasped at the sight of something behind Charisse. She grabbed the seat of her chair to keep from lifting off the ground. Charisse turned to give a puzzled look then disappeared down the hall.

"Aha!" Federline exclaimed. "So you see that too?"

"Get that thing out of my house! My daughter is upstairs!" my mother said in a hushed and exasperated tone.

"It's harmless to us. That's her curse. It has been following her since the first time it happened. But I must tell you something about your daughter."

"Fed, be careful. Be very careful."

"Here she is your blessing. When she leaves, she will be your curse in four years time."

My mother sat in the chair staring into space. Not one to ever be speechless, Federline obviously struck a nerve. He slowly rose from his chair and showed himself to the door. He had to give my mother time to digest what he said.

"And remember, Madame. I'm never wrong."

My mother would eventually realize how right he was.

I tossed and turned all night due to my anxiousness to begin college. I didn't feel nervous about meeting new people or adjusting to a new way of life because I would have two slices of home with me on campus. Thinking about it made me realize I had not spoken to Mari since the night she held her graduation party. I knew she felt torn between maintaining our friendship and being obedient to her mother, who had a penchant for keeping up appearances. In her mother's mind, my family were "those people" and not on her level, whatever she was deceived into thinking it was. However, Mari's father, Jacob Ingram, always acted as the buffer and never made me feel unwelcome in their home. He was a christian minister who was well-versed in the bible but didn't take it literally, unbeknownst to his fellow members. He used to be a religious studies professor at a christian college and was accused of heresy when he began to become more open expressing his real views, including the idea that there may be life in outer space. His argument was the bible never said Earth was the only place that had life, so why were we saying it? That type of thinking did not sit well with the college president so the college pulled a Galileo on him, which resulted in his forced resignation to save him the embarrassment of being fired. They felt it was the "christian" thing to do.

Because of her father's loose ideologies, Mari's household was very liberal in the sense that they embraced all philosophies. While I didn't believe in anything in particular, Mari believed in everything to the point where I would lose track of what were her core beliefs. It seemed whatever religion or ideology helped her through her tough time, that's what she was going with. But at the end of the day, she still called herself a christian. That vacillation made it more tolerable to be around her because she did not engage in the dogmatism most people who were religious did. Her problem was she just wanted me to believe in something, but my logical mind would not let me grope in the dark. Despite the religious open-mindedness that took place in the Ingram household, the night of my graduation party her father drew the line.

"Mari, you know I don't choose your friends for you. I leave it up to you to decide who is best for you, but your mother and I have to put our foot down about going to Suzi's graduation party. I know what those people do over there."

Her father was referring to my mother's activities, which everyone knew about but only spoke of in hushed tones. It was an open secret that hid in plain sight.

"Daddy," Mari explained. "Suzi is different. She doesn't believe in it."

"She might not believe in it, but she's affected. She got her mother's ways and she doesn't even know it. It's in her demeanor."

"But Daddy..."

"You don't have to practice witchcraft to be affected by it. Just be in the same house, around it, watching it. She's bewitched and I prayed all the prayers I can pray to keep you protected from it."

Mari's father went on to explain how spirits transfer and that they can get into a person's personality. He said the intent of witchcraft was intimidation and manipulation for the purpose of domination. My mother controlled people she never even met simply due to the threat of having to deal with her wrath.

"That night she attended your party, I saw something on her."

Mari's mother, Hilda, who stood silent throughout the conversation, placed her hand over her mouth and began to wring her hands.

"Honey! Don't share that. Please don't share that! Mari can't handle it."

"What can't I handle? She's my friend. I know her."

"Mari," her father continued. "She has three spirits on her; suicide, anger, and schizophrenia."

As soon as her father said those words, they heard the sound of glass breaking in Mari's room.

"NO!" her mother screamed. "NO! That's that woman in our house! She's in our house! Do something!"

Mari's father grabbed everyone's hand and began to pray. He prayed for protection over their home and rebuked whatever spirits he sensed were in his house to intimidate his family and stop him from speaking against me and my mother. When Mari told me the story some time later, I was inclined to believe her because she would never lie to me. At the same time, I felt it was a great plot by her and others to continue to discredit my mother. There was something in me that always made me ignore what people told me happened in my own home.

My recollection of events was interrupted by a series of moans from the spare room across the hall where Charisse slept. At first I thought maybe she was hungover and dealing with some nausea until I heard hard, fast breathing.

"I know that girl is not in there…," I said to myself as I jumped out of my bed to see what the commotion was. Before I put my hand to the door, it swung open and I saw two eyes staring at me. Neither one of us blinked but rather stood still waiting for the other to look off.

"Let me come in here," Charisse whispered. "It keeps coming for me."

"What keeps coming for you?"

"Nothing. Just let me sleep in here."

"Charisse, what are you talking about?" I demanded. "You're talking in code. You know I hate that."

Charisse just ignored me and climbed into my bed, pulled the cover over her head, and curled up in a ball.

"And I hate that too!" I said, noting how she would choose to pretend not to hear me in order to avoid more querying. "Now where am I supposed to sleep?"

I didn't have anything against sharing a bed, but the last time Charisse and I shared linens I woke up itching and scratching. My mother had to make a concoction of tea tree and olive oils to send the crabs back to the sea. She said Charisse had nasty girl's disease and she was banned from the house for a while. When she came back, she had to sleep in the spare room that my mother used to store her dolls. She had dolls of all sorts in that room. Big ones, small ones, ones that stared at you no matter what position you were in the room, and others that were shy and seemed to look away when you tried to make eye contact. My mother always made sure to put them away whenever Charisse spent the night, probably because she had a few in there that looked like her father and siblings. I wasn't sure since I rarely went into that room, but I did remember my mother purchasing some vintage Matchbox cars, removing some parts as though she was a tinkering mechanic, then putting them beside a bald doll in the room with the pieces scattered everywhere. When I asked what was the point in that, she replied, "Exactly."

"Why do we even put up with her?" my mother asked one day when Charisse called to say she was on her way to the house. "Her daddy ain't no good. Her mama, rest her soul wherever it is, was a nice lady but a dummy if I ever saw one. Her siblings act like a bunch of field niggas overdosing on Christmas molasses and scallions…"

"Eww, ma! That's nasty!" I said.

"And you nastier because that's your friend," she retorted. "I keep telling you and you don't listen. Birds of a feather flock together. Now what feathers you got that match hers? Search yourself, Small Suzi. Search yourself."

The recollection of a crab fest hosted in my very clean bedroom made me shudder, but I did not want Charisse to feel any worse than she felt earlier when I remarked about her traveling bags. I jumped in the bed with my back to her, eyes wide open because I decided to think about how our feathers possibly matched—or not. We were nothing alike outside of our loyalty to each other. She was loud, I was quiet. She liked attention, I loved the background. She felt everything and sometimes I felt nothing. We were everything the other wasn't, so I determined we were made for each other. Perfectly incongruent.

"Suzi, you up?" Charisse asked. It was a question she always asked whenever she spent the night. "I can't sleep."

"Seems to me like you should be sleeping good after all that racket across the hall. All you need now is a smoke—but not in here."

"Suzi, stop clowning. Listen, this is our last night before we go down South and I'm excited."

"Me too."

"I get to get out of that stupid house. I hate that house."

I listened intently as Charisse began to share her frustrations about living with her father and his raggedy children. It was not often that Charisse would intelligently explain her thoughts about her family situation. I always pieced together her narrative from the times she would run over to the house in trouble, or my mother would blurt something out against her father as though she were a scorned lover or that he owed her money. They had a funny relationship. My mother hated him to death but was always talking about him. Strange.

"Sometimes I feel like I want to kill myself," Charisse confessed.

"That's old news, girl. Get in line."

"You feel like that too?"

I didn't realize I let that little revelation slip as I was the strong one and could never show any weakness to her. I was the alpha female in the friendship and she was the beta. The day I needed her would be the day our friendship ended because our friendship couldn't function unless she needed me and not me her.

"Go on with your story," I dictated. "I'm just talking."

"Well, I don't understand why God cursed me. I feel cursed. I mean, my mama died when I was young. My father, well, he don't act like a daddy sometimes. I hate my brother and sisters. They tease me and stuff. They steal my clothes and use all my stuff I keep in the bathroom. I mean, I just have no peace in that house. I just want to be someplace where I can feel like I'm at home. I never felt like I had a home or a family. Even when my mother was alive, she was so busy with daddy and I felt like chattel."

"What?"

"Chattel. Social Studies word from slavery times."

"Oh."

I knew what it meant but I didn't anticipate it flying out of her mouth with such ease. I urged her to continue to purge. She had to get it all out before she left for college.

"Explain to me why you feel cursed. I mean, if there was such a thing as god, why would he do that to you?"

"I don't know. I mean, I feel like I never had a chance..."

"To breathe," I interrupted.

"Right. To breathe. That's what I want to say. I never had a chance to inhale or exhale love. I never had a chance to feel normal. I had to laugh all the time to hide my feelings. I date all these different guys from out of town to feel like I have something going on, but they use me too. That's why I'm over here all the time. This feels like a home."

"How you figure that? We have our own problems up in here. I mean, you know, it's just me and my mother. Sometimes Reesie rolls through and camps out."

"But y'all love each other. I mean, look at your room. It's straight out of a JC Penny catalog. You got curtains to match your bedspread and a real bedroom set. You missing the armoire, though. And you got clothes and shoes and nobody touches them. You always have food to eat, a 10-speed bike that makes that nice clicking noise when you stop pedaling, Barbie dolls that look like you, the house got three floors...you lucky. I'm not. I hate myself. I hate my life!"

I didn't know what to say to her because if I believed in god, I would say he cursed her too. Even though I knew she was not always happy at home, I never felt sorry for her. Rather, I felt she was built for that kind of life and would find a way to navigate it with a little help from friends. I did feel responsible for her, though, because we went way back like pigskin shoes.

"Charisse, I'll protect you and whatever I have, you have. You know that."

"I'm not tough like you, Suzi. You don't let nobody mess with you. You don't get interrupted in your sleep like I do. Sometimes twice in the night by both the yin and the yang."

"Charisse, if you are not ready to tell me something, just don't say it. You don't have to talk in code."

"But even when I do, you understand. You're smart. I'm not. I hate myself!"

One thing I always hated to do was assume. I liked things spelled out to the point where my mother questioned how deep was the rose tint in my glasses. It wasn't that I was oblivious to what people went through, but I preferred not to tell myself someone else's story. Or rather, stories I didn't want to hear.

"Hmmm," my mother said one day when Charisse was at the house. "Yep!"

I looked at her with a curious look then turned away because I knew it was at those moments my mother would begin to spout whatever sermon she had on her mind about something she'd been pondering for a little too long.

"Hmph, hmph, hmph!" she continued while taking a toothpick to the next level with her right hand, lips and teeth in sync with all the eyeball action. All the while my mother stared at Charisse, who had her back turned. Charisse most likely knew that my mother was remarking about her, but knew better than to turn around and ask what it was all about.

"Oooh wee!" my mother continued. "What a rascal! What-a-rascal! And the sister too? Hmph hmph hmph! Y'all a mess in that zoo. Suzi, excuse your mama right quick. I got another doll to make."

I never asked my mother why she needed to make another doll or what she meant by mentioning Charisse's sister. Sometimes I just didn't have a need for things to add up. And as I looked at Charisse lying in my bed for peace and safety, I wondered if she really was overwhelmed or if she was just a drama queen who needed to always be reminded that she mattered.

"We need to get some sleep. But let me tell you this, Charisse. After all that you say you feel and have gone through, for you to have the strength to get good grades and go to college says a lot. One thing you are not is dumb. You're naturally bright, but you just need some push and seasoning. Everybody got problems and everybody got to find a way to overcome them—you included. When you leave this town, reinvent yourself."

"Reinvent myself. Yea. Then I could upgrade the guys I pull! Thanks Suzi!"

We finally got to sleep, but it would not hold me for long. I tossed and turned all night, attributing my nightmares to anxiety about leaving home. I was half asleep and half awake while a horror movie was playing in my head.

"Charisse!" I screamed.

"What?" she groggily replied. Apparently only one of us was getting a good night's sleep.

"Nothing."

I didn't want to tell her I was dreaming about her. In the dream I watched Charisse through a glass door as she danced with a tall figure in a black tuxedo with a monogrammed handkerchief in his breast pocket. I could not make out the letters, but I knew the last letter was a "V". Charisse wore a blood red dress and swirled around the room as though she didn't have a care in the world. Flames were about her feet and it was as though the heat of the flames made her dance all the more. As soon as the figure pulled her towards him in a tight embrace, the dress burst into flames starting from the bottom, licked up her body while skipping her abdomen, and continued up to her head. I screamed and banged on the door to no avail, but I was clearly disturbing the person she was with. The figure finally turned around and I discovered it did not have the face of a man. It opened its mouth and a forked tongue shot out like a flame. He screamed, "Quittez-moi!"

When I realized what it was, I woke up and tried to scream but no sounds would come out of my mouth. I had a tingling feeling in my head like when my foot falls asleep, and I knew my mind woke up before my body, which meant I would have to jerk myself awake. If I tried to relax and fall back asleep, I was afraid of what I'd see. I finally broke free and screamed for Charisse. That was when my mother appeared at the door.

"Suzi,"

"It's alright. It's alright," I assured my mother. "It's alright."

"No it's not!" Charisse blurted out as she pulled the covers over her head.

"You two have to get up in a few hours and you know Reesie will be ready to ride. If you can't go to sleep, drink some warm milk and honey."

"She'll be sleeping and I'll be wide awake because she be firing off. She lacrosse intolerable!" Charisse volunteered.

"Lactose intolerant!" I yelled.

"Whatever it is!" Charisse retorted. "You be shooting liquid hell out of those hind parts, that's what I'm saying. We need a divider between us or something. A big bucket to bounce the sound. Or something!"

"Funny," my mother said while rubbing her chin. "I don't remember nobody named Charisse being addressed."

At that moment the crickets outside relished at the thought of being heard again as all of the actors on the set of my bedroom fell silent. The director had spoken.

"And by the way Suzi," my mother continued. "It was telling you to leave him alone."

"What are you talking about?" I asked in bewilderment, wondering if I screamed "quittez-moi" in my sleep.

"Good night," my mother said as she closed the door behind her.

In the deathly silence I had a sense of foreboding that came over me every time I looked at Charisse. I had never felt anything like it before, and it was as though my whole body was screaming to understand why the day before I was to embark on a new journey, I felt the person next to me would not go all the way. *Leave me alone.* Strange.

I thought I would have the opportunity to fall asleep again since we had only a few hours before we had to rise and shine, but someone else was apparently dreaming about Charisse that night because I heard a man's voice yelling outside in the yard.

"I know, I know, I KNOW this nigga is NOT in my yard yelling for this girl. I KNOW!"

My mother marched down the hall like she was the alpha elephant showing the rest of the herd how it's done—huge leather belt in hand with the buckle caressing the floor as the man outside kept screaming for Charisse.

"Charisse!" I yelled. "Is that your father outside yelling for you?"

She rolled over and looked out of my bedroom window which faced the front yard.

"Yup," she said as she peeled herself from under the covers and began to put on her clothes.

"Where are you going?"

"I have to go to him."

"What are you talking about? Go to him?"

Before we could continue our verbal volley, I realized that my mother was already outside confronting Charisse's father.

"You's a dumb fool, you know that? Dumb! You up in my yard yelling for a child? Are you stupid?"

"Esther, I want her home in my house. This ain't her house. Charisse!"

"In your house or in your bed, you dirty bald-headed spook!"

I watched Charisse's father teeter back and forth, clearly inebriated and not realizing my mother was about to change his name.

"Esther, I don't want no trouble."

"Do you know where you are? Do you know who you are standing before?"

"That's my daughter! She leaving and she ain't come home and I want to see her. Charisse! Ch…"

I pulled Charisse from the window and put my hand over her eyes. I did not want her to see her father getting whipped with the shiny end of a belt, but she was not to be tied down. Before I could grab her, Charisse was off and running outside to stop my mother from pummeling her father into sobriety. That was not the first time Charisse ran to rescue her father from being emasculated by my mother.

"Daddy! Daddy!" Charisse yelled. "Miss Esther, please!"

My mother stopped mid-whip and stared at Charisse with the most contempt I had ever seen. Her mouth did its best to stay shut, but the words eked out from between her clenched teeth as though they had to fight to make their presence known.

"If you don't get your rotten self back in that house, Charisse! Get up in there!" my mother said in a low growl.

"I got it from here, Miss Esther," a voice said from the edge of the lawn. It was Creepy. For some reason my mother had a respect for Creepy that she did not give anyone else. It was as though he were a kindred spirit, but just part of another generation.

"Don't you get yourself in no trouble, Creepy," my mother warned. "This is my quarrel."

"I got him, Miss Esther. You ladies have a good night."

Creepy put Charisse's father's arm around his neck and disappeared into the night towards the park. As the two got further and further away, we all heard a man screaming in the distance.

"That Creepy is something else!" my mother marveled. "I like that boy. Black as tar, but I like him."

All except my mother began to file back into the house as she stood where Creepy was when he had arrived. She turned towards the park and with one hand on her hip, she looked as though she were still watching him walk down the street.

"Let him go home now," she said in a volume that indicated he was standing next to her, except he wasn't.

"Ma!" I said. "Who are you talking to? Creepy's not here."

"Yes he is," she said pointing directly in front of her.

"Creepy is thataway," I retorted as I looked down the street where he vanished with Charisse's father.

"His *body* is at the park."

No doubt my mother was high on some really good stuff. I mean some *really* good stuff. I ended our conversation by turning my back and staring at Charisse who was watching us both banter about a friend, who I've known all of my life, being able to leave his body and be in two places at one time. If his ghost was standing on the lawn with us, who was in his body taking Charisse's father back home?

"I see your puzzlement," my mother began. "Let me tell you about that boy."

"I don't want to know nothing about that hocus pocus. He has nothing to do with all that stuff you do and he is not out of his body astral projecting or whatever you all call it. If anything, you are looking at a reflection that your eyes recorded due to the light."

I went on to explain to my mother how under the right circumstances, a person can see an object that used to be in a certain place because the sunlight, or a very bright light, recorded the image and her eyes picked it up. She proceeded to tell me that all the science in the world can't explain the truth I've been running from my entire life, that astral projection was real, and that if I weren't such a stubborn mule, I'd be following her in her footsteps.

"But for some reason you got something blocking me and I bet it's those Ingrams! Either them or them church women in Pentecost Sunday white! Either case, I'm dealing with it real soon."

"I don't believe in it, that's why!"

"That's a croc of bull, that's what it is. You don't *want* to believe in it with all your math and science. But you can't beat fate. You are next in line to carry these gifts and you will do it!"

I have heard those words before, except they were told to someone else when I was a child. I was about eight or nine when we made a stop in Haiti as part of a cruise to Jamaica where my mother's friend, Rita, was from. The island was beautiful, so much so that the cruise captain called it by another name as though it would be an insult to say it was part of the actual country of Haiti. We were supposed to just spend the day there and set sail at night, but something happened with the ship that did not allow it to leave until two days later. While the vacationers were in an uproar, Rita and my mother seemed quite happy that the ship obeyed their orders to stay put until we got back.

I remember a man meeting us who had long dreadlocks and a yarn cap with Rastafarian colors. He spoke with a heavy accent that sounded like he twisted his words every time he said something that began with a "th" or an "r". At times he vacillated into Kreyol, which my mother and Rita understood perfectly. At some points they even led the way as though they had been there many times.

We got to a small clearing and boarded a jeep that had mud caked on the wheels, no doubt from traversing back and forth into territory where people didn't go. There were little things dangling from the rearview mirror—things that looked like teeth, fur and skin. It was more like a bootleg Dream Catcher, except it looked more like it caught nightmares and returned them new and improved.

"Shame how they treat these people," Rita said.

"Yea, they too close to African. Isn't that right, Pierre?" my mother asked our escort.

"Mais oui, we are proud of our African heritage, our skin, our culture, our sun, our moon, our everything. Tout le monde want to be like us. Forte! Strong! Haitiain blood is strong blood!"

"Y'all need a little of that Spaniard them Dominicans got to soften you people up," my mother replied, totally ignoring Pierre's delight in sharing his heritage, one in which the world was afraid to accept. She learned from my light-skinned, color-obsessed grandmother that there was such a thing as black and *too* black, and that she hated both. However, we were in a country with a proud and rebellious history, one that apparently made it possible for her to visit and ride through washes of green that were like nature's gateways to another world. She had black and *too* black people to thank for that.

"Haiti is a diverse place like Yard," Rita explained, referring to Jamaica. "They have all colors here, but the ones on the bottom look like the ones on the bottom everywhere else. Take your ex-husband, for instance."

My mother rolled her eyes and changed the subject while Pierre seemed to enjoy any conversation that told the truth about his country.

"We are here ladies," Pierre announced after riding for an hour. We arrived at a place that looked like a small compound. There were people outside all dressed in long robes and twirling and dancing. They looked like strange beasts urging the sun to go to bed and to let the moon have a turn to spy on the world.

Mesmerized by the display of pure ecstasy in dance that was taken straight out of Pan's playbook, my mother dragged me inside as we had to meet Madame Samedie. She was a robust woman with caramel colored skin, well manicured feet, and breasts that lazily rested on her abdomen. She had a slow and deliberate stride like the slave women who walked one after the other down dirt roads with a hatchet in their hands. It was a walk that said they will cut The Man's sugar cane—and him too—if he broke the line.

Madame Samedie walked towards me like a grandmother who was happy to see me, except she had a young, smooth face that looked no more than fifty. As a child she was an old woman to me, but my young adult memory autocorrected and put time, place, and people in their proper perspective. She looked tall in her bare feet—tall enough to be a bully—but she was more of a gentle giantess with a smile that radiated like the sun. When she approached me, all I felt was warmth, peace, and welcome. When she touched my cheeks, I felt danger. I drew back and ran behind my mother.

"Qu'est-ce que c'est? What is it?" Madame Samedie said with much indignation.

"What do you mean?" Rita asked. "This is the girl."

"Can't be. I've been grooming her from afar since the failed attempt before she was born. I even come to her in her sleep. This girl does not know me."

Smart for my age, I understood that Madame Samedie was doing something that made her think we would be connected and that I'd recognize her upon first meeting. My mother began to query me to see if anything happened to me that I didn't tell her.

"Anything happen in your room, in your sleep, when you went to the toilet, anything? What you been dreaming, Suzi? Tell me!"

I recalled having dreams of a woman always coming into my room, but before she ever reached me, something would jump in front of her and I would wake up.

"Non! Non non non!"

"What's wrong, Madame?" my mother asked while Rita turned her head to avoid the wild look in my mother's eyes. "I been sending you money and all kinds of hair and skin, and whatever I could to get for this girl to get attached short of taking her blood, and you tell me you can't do it? You better call on every god and spirit guide you know! We ain't leaving here until this girl is primed! I need a successor or I'm going to die before my time!"

My mother shook her fists and stomped her feet, and it sounded like the whole world stomped in unison. If I could have seen invisible things, I would have seen the smoke that came out of her ears, eyes that turned red, and her jaws become a bigger threat than a bear trap. I heard the train that ran though her head whistle for all passengers to hurry and board before it not only pulled out of the station, but derailed on purpose. The next sound was that of a teapot threatening to drown the water if it was not taken off the stove right there and then. I had never seen my mother so afraid and angry at the same time, to the point where her hair looked like it was on fire.

Just as I thought things couldn't get any worse, a gang of little kids came into the room and began running circles around us. They were running and jumping and playing, and made noises that sounded like the buzzing of a swarm of angry bees. The noise became so loud that I began to violently pull at my mother's dress like I wanted to rape her clothes. Then my mother, or the lady who looked like my mother, grabbed me by the neck and was about to raise me off the ground when Rita intervened.

"Esther! Esther! Come to! Come to! Jesus, Lord have mercy!"

Although Rita practiced voodoo, my mother said when things got tough, Rita would call on the christian savior, which I found to be quite odd. Apparently the children thought it was odd as well because they began to scream at her and hurl threats for saying "that name" in their presence. They screamed and gnashed their teeth, and I saw that their teeth were like tiny razors. Then their faces changed, then their bodies, then even the very breath that came out of their mouths. The whole room smelled like sulfur and the ground shook as the children who turned back to little imps ran out of the room, except they did not use the door or a window.

Madame Samedie stood stock still and went into a trance. She began gyrating except only the trunk of her body moved like the waves of an ocean, a limp branch, or a thing that creepeth, and her limbs seemed to disappear. When she opened her mouth, a long tongue shot out as did the voice of a man with more authority than every god ever written about.

"Who is this you bring to me?"

"Monsieur," my mother said. "It's my child; my successor."

"I see the child. But who is with the child?"

"Monsieur, there is no one with this child."

"Liar! Rita! Qui est-ce avec l'enfant? Who is with the little one? Qui?"

Rita was afraid to answer his question about who I was because she mentioned "that name" and knew she would be called out on it by the man in Madame Samedie's body.

"Answer me!" the male voice said.

"Monsieur, she has people in her family. She has people who don't practice and we have been fighting them for her soul."

"Where are these people?"

"We don't know. They are relatives that stopped coming around before she was born. They moved away but said some things before they left. They worship…"

"Don't say that name in my ears!" the male voice said, except there were multiple voices that came out of Madame Samedie that time. "And you will answer for bringing him here! You, the mother, and the child! Get out!"

At the sound of "Get out!", Madame Samedie's head began to grow, and grow, and grow until it split into a row of four humps like a deformed camel's back. On each hump there was a face with different expressions. One was anger, another was a dumb spirit with saliva glazing its mouth, and the last two were volleying expressions of fear, torment, and pride between each other. All the while, old Madame Samedie's face kept changing into one or more of the expressions at breakneck speed to the point where she began to look even more terrified than the man in The Scream. She was trapped in her body and only her face could tell the truth when the other expressions stopped vying for an audience. But it was only for a millisecond at a time, and during that millisecond I thought I heard the young Madame Samedi, the person she was before the spirits made her answer her calling, scream, "Je veux retrouver mon vie! Sauve-moi!" But it was too late for her request to get her life back and be saved from her decision by anyone present. It was clear that the spirits were not interested in only a partial take over. In that world—her world, and my mother's world, and Rita's world, there was no democracy, no refunds, and no mercy. It was the definition of torment.

At the site of the heads collapsing, my mother fainted, Rita threw up, and I just stood staring at Madame Samedie as her body stopped waving as though it was steam rising from hot pavement. The heads folded like an accordion with the last expression telling me, "Soon!"

As the final act, Madame Samedie fell into a chair as the voice took all the vitality out of her body. Pierre came inside when he stopped hearing voices and scooped my mother off the ground like melted caramel. I was still holding my neck from where my mother choked my tonsils and was in so much disbelief that I convinced myself it was not real. And I had been convincing myself ever since.

"Snap out of it, you!" my mother screamed as she noticed I drifted off into a land far away from smoke and mirrors and into another land with even more smoke and more mirrors. "This is too much action for one night. Everybody get to bed, get to sleep, and get a dream or two. When Reesie pulls up later, I don't want to slap the taste out of her mouth for coming up in here rushing folks."

My mother offered me warm milk, honey, and a mixture of almonds, basil, and other items to help me relax and get to sleep. Charisse was knocked out cold as though Mike Tyson read her a bedtime story in the first round. I crawled into bed next to her and turned my back, barely brushing her ample rear that my mother said spread too soon for her age. I closed my eyes and listened to the cadence of Charisse's light breathing and wondered how could a person who went through so much sleep so well?

We woke up later that morning ready to rise and shine. As usual, Reesie was on time and ready to ride. She had Creepy in tow, who probably wanted to make sure he saw me off. A stickler for time, no doubt Reesie had some people in North Carolina waiting for her to show her the town after she dropped Charisse and me off to campus. As we were about to load, my mother took some green paste and rubbed it on my suitcases.

"This is to keep unwarranted actions away from you," she explained.

"And what about the warranted? You want me to get what I deserve?" I asked, knowing my mother would shoot back with something smart.

"You can handle that. You got fire in your blood. Whatever comes your way, you got it. That's how we do it in this house."

Reesie and Creepy had finished loading the car and my mother sensed Reesie's hand was about to hit the horn.

"Wait now! I'm seeing my daughter off!"

"Esther, you had all day and all night. I'm here. Let's go!"

"My daughter is going to college and you going to Hell! That's how we working it this morning? Touch the horn and see what happens."

Reesie lightly beeped the horn for spite and made sure my mother saw her laugh because she knew Esther was not one for idle threats. She was going to make good on it, even if it meant she'd have to flatten all of Reesie's tires and drive me down South on the back of a broomstick. Despite the minor antics, everyone knew it was time to go. True to form, my mother gave me parting words to live by.

"Remember all that I taught you. This will be your first time away from me for a long time. Nobody knows you're Esther's daughter down there so you have to do your own scrapping. Don't let nobody mess with you, hear me? When I send you money, don't flash it. Put it in the bank and be quiet with your spending."

"Ma, I know all this stuff."

"You know it because I told you, so shut up and listen again."

"I'ma let you finish."

"Let me finish what? Saying what I gotta say or finish pouring a cup of milk to put your front teeth in so they don't die en route to the emergency room? You following? Finish my advice or finish plotting which hand I'm going to use to catch the taste I'm gonna slap out of your mouth?"

"Ma, you're so violent!"

"Will you two angry, balled-up fisted, such and suches hurry up!" Reesie hollered.

"And last," my mother continued as she rolled her eyes a full 360 degrees, "I told you before and I will tell you again, when you get down to that campus, I don't care how long y'all been friends, you cut that little trick-or-treater Charisse loose, you hear me? She's a liability. A friendship built off of one rescuing another is not a friendship; it's a dependency. And that friend of yours, Daffodil..."

"Marigold!"

"Dandelion, Iris, Violet, Chrysanthemum, Ragweed, Cannabis, whatever! Mind people who think they're better than you and your family. Mind them!"

"Mari don't think...,"

"No, *you* don't think!" my mother interrupted. "That girl will die first before she utters a word to anybody in this family besides you. I don't like her, I don't like her family, and I don't like her kind. Period."

By the time my mother finished telling me the same things she'd told me for all of my life, Reesie blew the horn for real. To my surprise, Creepy was in the passenger seat to accompany us on the ride. Knowing my mother, she made him ride with us because she didn't trust Reesie on the road with precious cargo by herself. She thought Reesie was slightly dingy and four tires short of a unicycle.

I gave my mother a short hug—not being one for hugging—and watched her pretend not to cry. She reluctantly gave Charisse a hug, which Charisse was glad to receive. She was grateful to my mother and me for making sure she left for college in one piece with all of her belongings, a peaceful mind, and nothing in her womb. We both got in the back of the truck and watched my mother watch us fade away into the unknown. As Reesie drove further down the block, I could see my mother step off the sidewalk and into the street to continue watching us before we melted into the scenery around the corner. I tried to hold it in, but I shed a few tears for reasons I was both sure and unsure about. I turned over Federline's statement to my mother that in four years time I would be her curse. Despite my desire to tuck away all things uncomfortable, *that* I believed. I would find out in due time the price of belief.

# 2 EXODUS

The first three years of my time at college were uneventful. Apart from a few issues here and there that all college kids went through, I became comfortable believing that no bad predictions were likely to come to pass. Mari and I were able to maintain our friendship without interference from her parents, although I kept my mother's words in the back of my mind. I did not adhere to her directive about Charisse, who dove headfirst into a pool of testosterone and quickly built a reputation for herself as a loose person. For whatever reason, maybe stubborn pride or pure naiveté, I did not think for one minute that my reputation would be affected by what she did. No one saw me in bed with anyone or doing any of the things Charisse was rightfully accused of. However, in college it was not about what people saw you do but rather what they heard you might have done because of the person you were with who did.

Despite my dual reputation amongst a few amateur gossips, I managed to have my name cleared through keeping my nose clean outside of a few run- ins with stuck up people and disrespectful oafs, and because people eventually saw the disparity between Charisse's and my behavior. Not only that, but they eventually began to question if I liked men at all because I chose not to date anyone on campus. I was fiercely private and anything anyone knew about me outside of my small family and best friends wasn't because I told them. I had a few interests off campus with guys from other schools, but they always liked me more than I liked them because I was hard to get yet easy to talk to. My mother raised me to know all that both a man and a woman knows so that I could talk about anything from flagrant fouls to fragrant flowers. They had some of my attention and time, and maybe even a hand on a late night stroll, but never my heart. I didn't need to give it away or ever felt the need to. The closest I ever came to a boyfriend was Creepy and our connection was unspoken. It had no beginning or end; it just was.

It wasn't until my senior year that strange things began to happen to me that made me think more and more about the last words I heard Federline say. I began to have nightmares on a regular basis and would wake up not being able to move. My thought life became antagonistic towards anyone who said a word about religion, and on Sundays I didn't leave room for anyone to talk to me. My incidents seemed to coincide with the commencement of a new campus ministry and ironically, I had my first episode in my sleep on campus when they had their first service.

I remember having a bad dream and feeling like I was being suffocated. I kept trying to scream for help but no one would come. I was in and out of consciousness and not being able to fully wake up because I couldn't move, and yet afraid to fully fall asleep because the tingling feeling in my head would pull me back into the nightmare. The whole scene reminded me of Rita's claim that she could visit people in the night. It even reminded me of Madame Samedi. I thought that somewhere deep in my subconscious my body was playing out her words. The only way I was able to jump out of my paralyzed state was to think really hard, which would jolt me wide awake. I would have to sit up and let the blood in my body flow from my head to my feet before I could lie back down. The slightest tingle would make me sit back up for fear of falling back into a nightmare.

I was afraid to tell my mother what was going on because I knew she would have some supernatural explanation for what happened. I was in no condition to find myself in a jam that could only be fixed with more jams. It had to be the stress of school or not having the sense of unpredictable predictability that marked my home life. Mari suggested I see the school psychiatrist.

"I know you are not into church, so I suggest you get counseling," Mari advised. "You've been complaining about this for a while. It seems like your stress triggers it, because you didn't deal with this that much at home."

I was too mentally disjointed to respond because I could not wrap my brain around the loss of control I had over my own thoughts at night.

"I knew this was going to happen," Mari added.

I gave Mari a strange look that let her know she needed to explain herself and quick. Despite knowing my temperament, she was swift to continue her analysis of me.

"I know that you don't believe in the stuff your mother does, but I understand it to be real, and while you think you are immune to it because you don't believe in it, there is no way you can be around that and not be affected."

"So what are you trying to say? That I'm crazy?" I asked.

"What I'm saying is something is happening with you that is stronger than before. At home you were the Suzi everyone knew who was laid back but could be off the chain when she got ready. Here you have become more withdrawn, almost brooding and thinking all the time. You don't even smile."

"Have I ever smiled?"

Mari knew that was an honest question and she wasn't quite sure how to answer it. Smiling to keep from crying was not a smile, so I could not offer one.

"Mari, I'm just saying counseling doesn't work for me. You know black folks don't…"

"I don't want to hear all of that black this and black that."

"My mother said psychiatrists are for white people."

"And what's for black people? I would say church, but you don't believe in that."

"Black people work it out at home. We take some Tussin and sit in the back room for a few years until we get it off us. No counseling. I'll be back."

"You are way too smart to think like that."

I had to go out for some air to weigh what Mari said. I did not want to go to counseling because I had confidence that all I had to do was sit it out. I wasn't going to church because that was not my thing and my mother made sure it wasn't. I often looked up at the sky to ask it to tell me what was on the agenda for me in the grand scheme of the universe. And in my haphazard quest to find the answer, the sky finally replied back in the form of one of those campus bible thumpers who was part of the new campus ministry. I saw her around campus over the years and knew she was a christian, but when the new ministry came in, that was when she really began bouncing around campus like she didn't have a care in the world.

A lot of people didn't like her; it was probably more fear than anything. She didn't do anything to deserve to be hated, but I fell in with the crowd by shooing her away with dirty looks before she would open her mouth and say a robotic and annoyingly cheerful, "Praise the Lord!" I hated when she said that. The word "lord" didn't sit too well with me at all.

Despite her sunshiny ways, the Holy Sanctified Girl—as everyone called her—didn't truly look like she had anything to be happy about. Someone was obviously controlling her. She had this look in her eyes—a look of feigned happiness I was used to seeing on other christians that said, "I'm happy because I'm told I'm supposed to be, not because I am." Despite that autopilot look of hers, I decided to invite her into my world for a little bit to play with her. I was ready to strike with such precision that she'd probably question herself after leaving my presence. However, it was she who struck first and commenced to change my life.

"Praise the Lord!"

I mumbled "Whatever" under my breath then proceeded to commit to my task. "So how do you know jesus is real? You can't see him or anything. I mean, with all these religions out here, how can you tell someone he is the only way?"

I waited for her to recite some scripture her pastor told her would act as sinners' kryptonite, or tell me something she just learned in Sunday school and had not yet digested. I thought she would become frustrated and realize I was cornering her, but she just stood there with her hands folded with the same plastic smile she always wore.

"I know he's real because he lives in my heart. I know he's real because when I read the Bible and live according to it, my life continuously changes in ways it hadn't before. I know Jesus is real every time I am tempted to be my old self and yet I make a decision to keep being the new person that I am. That's how I know."

"Okay, well that's true for you but it might not be true for me."

"If you are sincere about believing in what's true, God will find you. And when he finds you, you must be ready to respond. Are you ready to accept Jesus into your heart today?"

"No, not quite. You still haven't convinced me."

"That's not my job. My job is to present you with the truth. Your job is to respond to it."

"Yea, but...."

"Have a good day!" she interrupted as she walked off in a brisk motion and adjusted her knapsack without being tempted to look back at me.

Even though I didn't buy what she said, I was left with a weird feeling. I thought she was going to give me the religious okey doke, the whole speech about Mary and Joseph and the manger, paying tithes, and stuff like that. But what she told me was that she was a different person. I wondered what she was really like before all of the Sunday this and that. What would make a person think anything could change them but themselves to the point where they would alter their entire lives for it? Instead of feeling the triumph of putting the Holy Sanctified Girl in her place, I felt a little intrigued. I needed a second, more in-depth conversation. I had to return to Mari's room and share the encounter, as she was more familiar with the organized side of religion in terms of the part that dealt with adhering to regular customs and rituals. In my household, religion was more like a quilt—patches of everything that didn't really go together, but nonetheless they were joined.

Because Mari was not what I would call a fanatic, I was open to hear her talk about bible stories and things that happened in church when she chose to go. Sometimes I would challenge Mari because I used to read the bible so that I could prove it wrong. I knew that by going to school in the South I would be faced with bible thumpers from every corner of the state. However, Mari never took offense to those debates because she knew the origin of my questions. In her estimation I never had a chance to respect religion because all I saw was manipulation and people dancing for the devil in my basement. I only had two frames of reference for christians, such as the ones my mother talked about as "them women in Pentecost Sunday white" who she had more contempt for than Democrats had for Republicans, and Liberals for Conservatives. The second batch was liberal christians like Mari's family who did not judge you if you were not one of them, but only did so if you were against them like my mother was. All of the others I just lumped into an unidentifiable, monolithic blob of people who went into a building and came out with the same clothes, the same bibles, and the same look of weekly obligation that they had when they walked in.

The question I had was why did Miss Holy Roller take religion so seriously to the point where she seemed to disconnect herself from the general population and talked about jesus more times than she took a breath? Although I had no interest in her personally, I had an interest in the different way that she seemed to live. She was never in drama, was oblivious to all insults hurled at her whenever she would try to do what they called "witnessing" on campus, and she was adamant about being the first one to open the church doors. Mari never spoke to her either, but I figured she could still help me sort my little conversation out.

"What did you say, girl? I don't believe it!" Mari exclaimed as I shared with her my brief conversation with Our Lady of Grace. "What in the world made you want to talk with her when you didn't even want to hear what I had to say all these years?"

"Ah, I don't know. I just wanted to pick on someone and she came along. I was in the mood for a fight."

"That's your problem right there! Always mad about something."

I couldn't deny my combative nature at times due to my readiness for whatever came my way. To be honest, I was becoming tired of it— so tired that I slipped up and talked religion. But I couldn't help myself. I couldn't keep wearing Mari out with my many questions and lack of emotional discipline at times, and I couldn't keep wearing myself out either.

Mari was in a talkative mood, proceeding to tell me that maybe I should take up Holy of Holies on her offer to accept jesus just to see if he could help me with my anger problem, or better yet, read some new book she picked up about meditation and using crystals to drain my negative energy, making my thoughts float away in some big imaginary balloon filled with helium. But I thought, it might explode like the Hindenburg, revealing the muck and mire that had to be hidden in my heart—things that had been building up for years in my mother's house that I refused to admit were real. Then that would also mean I'd explode again, like I do at times. I'd be back at square one as a hot, brown, gooey mess splattered all over Mari's lavender fresh room.

As Mari talked, all I could see was her mouth moving like she had ten of them, and the more she talked the more I slipped away. I kept staring at her boca grande, her canine teeth looking more canine by the second as she continued to dissect me. And the more she dissected what she thought was my problem, the more the color red began to dominate my mood. I just wanted to talk about my day and she wanted to put me on the couch. I was tired of her slicing away at my world with that scalpel of hers. When she hit an artery revealing fresh red blood, I had to cry out.

"Hey! Enough already!" I shouted suddenly.

"Enough of what? I was just telling you what I think you need some help with. You act like we didn't talk about this earlier."

"Ok, well next time let's talk about *you*!"

Maria drew back as though the thought of shifting the conversation from me to her, and putting herself in the position of the one to be advised was a terrible thought. And in our case, it would be because that was a role I didn't play; at least not in her life. Everyone needed someone to play second fiddle. It had to be someone who doesn't need as much as they are needed. I was to her what Charisse was to me, and at that moment the realization didn't feel too good.

Instead of walking out in a huff and leaving Mari offended by my outburst, we both just sat in the room looking at each other, wondering if we should have ever had that conversation. My eyes wandered all over the room looking for something to fixate on in order to distract me from dealing with my friend's analysis of my life. When I couldn't find anything, I had to conjure up something in my mind. Maybe a good memory, or maybe I could meditate on paying someone back who did something to me. I thought about the store clerk who ignored me and helped the customer that looked like him instead. In my mind I picked up a gun and shot him. I thought about the sorority sister who invited Mari to the Rush but said nothing to me. I pulled her by the hair and swung her around. My mind kept playing back the memory of my aunt's boyfriend who beat her in front of me, and when I tried to intervene, my aunt had enough strength to slap me for thinking of putting my hands on him. Then my mother found out and called her over to the house just to slap her back. After I finished with the store clerk and the alpha beta gamma delta girl, I shot the boyfriend too. I didn't give time for the gun to cool before I decided to turn it on myself. In real time my body jerked, causing Mari to give me a look. It was a nonchalant one that read she knew the drill.

"Did you die this time?"

"Whatever."

With that I decided to take up my huff and walk out without saying goodbye. I took it for granted that Mari would bounce back from my rudeness. At the time I didn't care if she did or not; I was irritated and wasn't ready to hear the things she said. I didn't want to hear that I had to take responsibility for my feelings, let things go, and learn how to calm down and trust someone else for a change. Trust someone else? Was she trying to say she was tired of being the only one I trusted? I had a mind to accommodate her, but I didn't have the strength to do it, and I didn't have the humility needed to crawl back to our friendship if I was wrong. I also didn't want to hear that I couldn't keep playing the victim, that at some point I had to realize maybe I was a victimizer. People didn't understand that I needed to be a victim. The world owed me for what it did to me. I didn't owe anyone anything but what they deserved. I was doing alright for three years and then out of nowhere I seemed to grow horns.

As I walked across campus, I enjoyed the breeze on my face and the wind talked to me in some kind of way. I didn't know what it was saying, but it sweet-talked me every time it brushed past my ears. I felt myself calming down and my favorite song kept playing in my head, the notes taking me up with the next current, lifting me up to the sky, high above my cares. I noticed every shade of blue, each one representing degrees in my life, degrees of pain, sadness, anger, sometimes joy. But, that joy came sparingly. Each cloud took shape, not the usual cat or dog people often saw, but rather celestial busts of people in my life whom I needed to tell me I would be fine. One even looked like jesus.

"jesus, is that you?" I asked sarcastically. "If so, you need to come down here and see about me. How 'bout it?"

As soon as "how 'bout it" left my mouth, a gust of wind came with a force that clearly communicated that it was trying to prove itself. This time it didn't just pass my ears, but rather my whole body. Before I knew it, I was picking myself up off the ground and staring at the wind in human form with plastic apologies written all over her face. It was HER.

"Praise the Lord! We meet again!" she greeted as she helped me wipe the dust from the ground off my pants, the same dust that probably made Adam and Eve. In my desire to float into the sky and chase those helium balloons from earlier that day, I didn't watch where I was going and missed a step, falling into Joanne the Baptist's knapsack. On the way down in an effort to stop my fall, I snatched open one of her pockets and small papers flew everywhere. How ironic that they were bible tracts. And it was also ironic that she did not lean back when I fell towards her, unlike Creepy did with Charisse that night in the backyard.

"I'm so sorry" she apologized.

"It was my fault," I conceded.

"It was, but it's okay. There's no such thing as an accident, you know."

I looked up at the jesus cloud to roll my eyes and shake my fists only to find it was no longer there. Maybe he did come down.

"Hey, why don't you take one of these and read it? I picked some up after our conversation earlier today and thought of you. You know I prayed we'd have the chance to talk again. We've passed each other for years and never spoke. God is so good right now!"

I really wasn't in the mood to say much, but I had to admit this chance meeting so soon didn't seem like chance.

"You know," she continued. "I never introduced myself."

I was really ready to hear this thing.

"It's Delilah."

"De what?" The look on my face said it all. The right side of my mouth curled up in an effort to suppress the biggest laugh ever.

"Delilah Jones. And you?"

"Suzi," I said tersely.

"What's your last name?"

"Just Suzi."

Undeterred, Delilah sans Samson offered me the bible tract and I reluctantly took it. It was a small two-sided reading about the holy spirit and being "born again". On the front was a picture of the sky and underneath there was a bible verse, John 3:8, "The wind bloweth where it listeth, and thou hearest the sound thereof, but canst not tell whence it cometh, and whither it goeth: so is every one that is born of the Spirit." I begged the right side of my mouth to suppress the gasp dying to escape me. I stood stock still for so long that I began to look like the column Samson knocked down after he was blinded by Delilah.

"If you want to learn more, we're having Bible study tomorrow night in the Student Center. It's at 7 p.m."

I didn't answer with my mouth. I suppose it was tired from holding all of my emotions in for a change. I simply answered by walking away. I felt it was nonsense. Pure nonsense. If jesus was toying with me, I was not amused. I wanted him get back in that cloud.

I became Creepy in a dress and walked around campus aimlessly— furious for no reason. The religion thing got under my skin and it wasn't even Sunday. There was something about people who made religion their entire lives that I just couldn't understand, especially at a time in life when a person is supposed to experience the normal rites of passage most people go through in their younger years. I could see if a person was a minister or some type of preacher. They were *supposed* to walk around in Pentecost Sunday white every day. But average people going to school or walking the dog? I just didn't see the seriousness of the fervor. Maybe they thought they were going to die soon, or were guilty of something and gave their lives to god to feel better about themselves. Strange.

I remember the first time I ever set foot in a church I was with Mari because my mother never took me to any religious edifice or even discussed anything outside of spirits and something in the sky. She took great care to make sure I never settled on any particular ideology, especially christianity. She used to always talk about the "women in white" who were "holy rollers" and went into trances and started talking really fast like they were at an auction. She seemed to have a fixation with a certain shade of white, almost to the point of hatred. She said those christians wearing white was hypocrisy at its finest because nobody was pure and nobody was changed. Despite my mother's protests, I found it hypocritical of her since she often wore pure white during her basement parties. Sometimes she's wear blue or red from head to toe, but most times she had at minimum a white scarf on her head. Maybe she thought the christians desecrated her shade of white.

My first time in church was a Friday night christmas program Mari invited me to with hopes that I'd be entertained while learning what the essence of christianity was about. At that time I was staying over Reesie's house as I often did when she was in between boyfriends. That particular weekend Reesie was holed up in the house with some man who she was thinking of graduating to "uncle" status, which meant I had to crash somewhere until the weekend tryst was over. I did not want to alert my mother that Reesie put me out for a man. Also, I was not one to protest getting out of the house, so I gladly let the two dopamine addicts have the place to themselves while I spent time with my best friend. Mari's mother reluctantly let me spend the night after service, citing with her haughty looks that she was not too keen on having people who were outside of their social class in the house. Mari's family were middle class Negroes who went bust but acted like they still had money because they kept all the signs of wealth like the nice car, house, clothes, and furniture. The fact that they lived around people who were not as privileged as they were seemed to give them license to act superior. Her father, however, was not so bad. Even though he had signs of stuffiness—probably from his affiliations with academe and belonging to the "Doc Club" at church—he was okay with people in the house. I suspected it was to show that he was able to have his family live well when the reality was when the church stopped giving, there was no good living.

Even though thievery was the furthest thing from my mind, I surveyed Mari's house as though I would return one night with a sack and a ski mask. The house was tastefully decorated in antique furniture and the walls were ornamented with gold leafing and crown molding. My mother always told me that a sign of a good home was crown molding. There were pictures everywhere of family members, degrees on the wall, three preaching licenses from different christian denominations, and all sorts of stuff that read, "Look at me." It was in stark contrast to my house which, while clean and well-kept, had no familial touches. There were only pictures of me around the house and various masks that were supposedly used in rituals in foreign countries. There were no photos of my mother, Aunt Reesie, and definitely no one from before my mother's generation out in the open. All of that seemed normal to me and I never cared to ask why. However, that lack of connection to family memories made me somewhat stoic at times and when surrounded by the opposite, I became uneasy. And while at Mari's, the uneasy seeped out of my pores like old, stifled sweat that was glad a hot day finally arrived to set them free.

"Is your family going to stare at me all night?" I asked, annoyed by the display of smiling faces on the walls and everything with a flat surface.

"It's just pictures, Suzi," she answered. "Don't tell me you're paranoid."

"No, but you people overdo it. I mean, you know you got family. You don't have to prove it to everybody. Half of those people probably don't come over anyway."

"You don't have family come over your house?"

"We're best friends. Why don't you know that?"

As usual, Mari ignored my random rants and resumed whatever she was thinking or doing before I began. She had a weird way about her, almost like she could see through me and was thus never surprised by me. She would say whatever she had to say then leave the ball in my court to figure it out. And while I would attempt to figure it out, I would always return to her to put her through another round of my insecurity just to hear her tell me what I had to think about. I was a sucker for direction because for all of my life, my inner compass spun in endless confusion. At that rate I was on track to become perpetually lost and thus discover a thousand Americas.

It was eventually time to go to church, which meant it was time to change into an acceptable outfit that would help me get seated close to the front. Not knowing what I was expected to wear, I brought with me two dresses Reesie bought me from Italy. One of her boyfriends purchased it for her as a gift for supposedly getting my mother to put some kind of hex on his business competitor, which he believed actually worked. My aunt, being a label chaser, always made sure I had something just right for every occasion so that no niece of hers would ever leave the house "looking like a barrel of monkeys and who done it."

"Where'd you get that?" Mari's mother asked once we emerged from the room dressed and ready to go.

"I think my mother got it from a consignment shop," I lied.

"Oh. Well you know that is a very expensive garment you're wearing—that is if it's not a knock off. Have to be careful with those thrift shops, you know."

"Yea, it probably is fake," I replied.

I was not going to fool myself to assume she didn't think Mari was the only one who could have something, therefore keeping up the façade that she was the alpha female in all of her friendships. Unlike Mari, I did not have someone at home teaching me to be better than everyone else. There was something about just being me that was more attractive than keeping up appearances. Nevertheless, I admired Mari for somehow being chosen to represent for the pseudo-elite. And whatever part I could play in maintaining that dynamic was okay with me.

Despite my efforts to make sure I had the right outfit, once we arrived to church I found my fears were unfounded. Surprisingly—and I'm sure to her mother's dismay— Mari went to a church with a mixed congregation, and from what I've heard, usually those type of churches did not have the same pomp and circumstance black churches had. Thankfully my clothing, while fashionable, was not frilly and accented with all kinds of stuff that could be pulled off by a curious toddler. I also had no hat, matching gloves, or scarf. And despite looking nice, we did not wind up in the front because Mari's church, Lakeside Open Arms Church, practiced what her father called "religious socialism", which was a souped up term for egalitarianism. The front row was reserved for whoever arrived first. The only people who were guaranteed choice seating were special guests or those serving in the church and needed easy access to wherever they needed to be. I saw no seats behind the pulpit that I was used to seeing on TV shows and movies, which Mari explained was something unique to her church. Her pastor preferred to sit facing the same direction as the congregation so that he would be able to participate in the service the same as everyone else. He did not want to be viewed as someone who was just waiting to speak for an hour.

Thankfully the service that night was more about the christmas play than telling people how they needed to go to church. Despite my head being filled with anti-christian rhetoric for most of my life due to my mother's fear of a certain shade of white, I was somewhat neutral that night. I did not leave there with the impression that there was something I had to do to alter my life or that I was going to hell. It was a nice night with my best friend that did not put me for or against church any more than I already was. I had heard the story of baby jesus so many times that I was not afraid of it. For me, baby jesus would always remain in a manger because I was not looking for him to grow up; at least not in my life. And judging from the mixed beliefs Mari's father taught her, jesus was only conveniently real.

What I did hear that night that impressed me was something I did not equate with religion. At the end of the service, the pastor got up and talked about how following jesus was a path to an improved version of who you already were. Instead of preaching that people had to change, he made it sound more like you were okay the way you were, but that you just needed to get better at some things. It made me think of how my mother talked about the christians she knew before they became one, and how they turned into completely different people overnight, personalities and all. She would call it a puppet show and declare, "Ain't nobody never putting their hand up my dress calling themselves moving me every whichaway!"

After arriving back to Mari's house, we stayed up all night talking, listening to music, and looking through magazines pretending different celebrities were people close to us. I chose them for friends and children, while Mari had the nuclear family, social clubs, and domestics. She pointed out that I needed to choose a husband before I chose the kids. I simply replied, "I turned out fine," and kept flipping the pages on the hunt for a set of twins with thick, fluffy hair.

"So are you going home in the morning or coming to church again with us?" Mari asked.

"Once is enough, don't you think? The play was good, but you know I don't believe in that stuff."

"You know enough about it, though. Probably more than a lot of people who go to church every day."

"Yea, but that's because I read and we talk about it sometimes. I am not trying to practice all that stuff in there. That's the part that confuses me—when the book comes out of the book and people take it seriously. Anyway, you know how my mother feels about christians. She told me to stay away, so I stay away. If she knew I went to church with you, she'd come over here and burn the place down."

"But doesn't your mother practice something? I mean, those people you told me about that come to the house with those head wraps and tambourines and stuff. I heard..." her voice trailed off as though she were about to commit a serious friendship violation.

"Heard what?" I asked, leaning in close so that I could hear her slip up about my mother.

"Isn't your mother a fortune teller or something?"

She just spit it out like she was telling me my mother was a venerated saint.

"Or something," I said, returning to my magazine to resume my fruitless search for my elusive twins. "But I bet I can tell you what your mother is, though, seeing how I'm here all the time."

"Here's your twins!" Mari said triumphantly. The Olsen twins were not what I had in mind.

My trip down memory lane was interrupted by an all too familiar, albeit annoying, voice from a friend.

"Girl, you need a drink!" Charisse yelled in my ear loud enough for the whole world to hear. "It's time to celebrate! Two more months and we are outta here for good! Yea girl! You look a little stiff tonight. What's up with that? Never mind. You always look like that."

I should have known better than to pass Charisse's dorm on the way back to mine. She was always outside hanging with a bunch of guys, loud and carrying on like they were amused by her. Even though she was also my best friend, I was not in the mood to deal with her. I needed to be in a quiet space. For that reason, I insisted on always having my own dorm room from day one.

"Yo Suzi! Whaddup playa?" one of the guys in the dorm yelled from his room window. "We're playing Spades up here. Roll through."

Before I could answer, Charisse already had me by the hand to lead me through the door. She had a crush on this guy but he never gave her the time of day. I was her excuse to get in his good graces and I knew what I had to do. After we finished playing the game, I had to pretend I had something else to tend to, leaving Charisse opportunity to work what she thought was magic.

Once we were inside, I was taken aback by the smell of marijuana, alcohol, and dirty sheets. Naziir, the host, pulled up two milk crates for Charisse and me to sit while we waited for his opponents to eventually lose. I kept staring at Naziir and wondered why Charisse would think a guy like him would ever want her. She was nice looking and all, but she was loud and sometimes obnoxious. Naziir was the epitome of cool, straight out of Brooklyn. He was one of those brothers who read up on everything and who people considered "conscious". He was the type who obeyed dietary laws, listened to Bob Marley, and didn't disrespect women. I was one of the few females he would have real conversations with because all the others wanted him for different reasons. Naziir and I had a lot of classes together and were sometimes study partners. Our friendship was birthed out of necessity versus attraction. This made me the object of envy of a lot of females on campus, but little did they know I wasn't checking for him that way.

"So what's new Suzi Q?" Naziir asked. Even though I didn't like him any more than I liked other guys I spoke with on campus, I did love the way he said Suzi Q. It made me blush and kind of forget my annoyances of the day. Charisse noticed and gave me a hard look.

"I'm good," I replied shyly, trying not to sound too excited in order to make Charisse feel comfortable. I had to be very careful. She was just as volatile as myself. While I erred on the side of anger, she erred on the side of weepiness and jealousy. The least little thing would cause her to sputter a volcano of tears and venom.

"How's your girl Goldie doing?" he asked, speaking of Mari.

"She's good," I said, still conscious of Charisse.

"You know she still ain't giving up the digits. What's up with that?" he said jokingly, knowing full well Mari had a boyfriend back home and no intentions of letting him go. I tried to change the subject because I knew Charisse was jealous of Mari, although she wouldn't admit it. Mari was exceptionally pretty and had all the features guys looked for.

Lost in thought again, I was interrupted by someone yelling, "Next victims!" and a female hand putting a beer and peanuts in front of me. It was our turn to play. We were shuffling and dealing until the wee hours of the night. It was Thursday night and nobody cared about Friday classes the latter half of the semester.

Between slapping cards on the table, drinking, and others passing the peace pipe, I began to totter. I wasn't sure if I was a little tipsy, high from breathing in all that Bob Marley air, or what. I looked around the room and there were at least six or seven guys present and a couple of females I didn't know. I knew it was time to stop playing and head back to my room.

"Alright, after this I have to bounce," I announced. Charisse looked disappointed. "Charisse, you better find your shoes."

"No. Leave your girl here. She's alright," Naziir protested. At that moment I have never seen her look so happy, but I was not leaving her there because if I was feeling tipsy and knowing how she loved the barley, she was probably on her way to being drunk, too.

"No, uh uh. She has to go back to her room. We came together and we have to leave together. Right, Charisse?" She gave me that "Why you blocking?" look. I realized I wasn't following the plan to leave her in the room with Naziir, but for whatever reason I felt I couldn't go along with it.

"I'll make sure she gets to her room," one of the guys in the room, Vince, volunteered. "I mean, it's only a few flight of stairs."

Still not convinced I should leave her, I gave Charisse one last look. By then she had turned her attention away from Naziir and was focused on Vince. I already knew what happened. Somewhere in between passing the peanuts and the beer, someone was passing signals that went beyond a game of cards. To my disappointment, Naziir was obviously in on it because he was the first to speak up.

Clearly realizing I was outnumbered, I went against my better judgment and left Charisse behind hoping—praying even—that she wouldn't fall into the wrong hands. In addition to being loud and obnoxious, she was also a little too trusting, which was my nice way of saying she was stupid when it came to men. Even though Naziir was cool, he probably wouldn't get in the way of one of his homeboys trying to hook up. I guess I was the only blocker in the room.

As I walked out, I began to get this sick feeling that something bad was about to happen. The scene of everyone happy and carousing, and Charisse with a sly look of eros love on her face, seemed like a weird juxtaposition against my thoughts. Not one to believe in intuition, the day had been so strange that I almost went with the feeling. But, my analytical side kicked in and assured me I had been spooked out by a jesus cloud and Delilah. Surely I had to find a way to return to normal.

Instead of going back to my dorm, I went down to the lobby and sat in the lounge. There were a couple of people watching television, a couple more minding their business, and one guy who decided to fixate on me in between words with his friends.

"Yea, that's her."

"Don't look like his type."

"Please! Not her. The friend."

"Who? Cherry?"

"Yea."

I knew they were talking about Charisse, but I was in no mood to defend her honor or even myself. I wasn't Naziir's type and he wasn't mine. Whatever ignited their conversation, Charisse deserved it. I didn't know how many times Mari and I told her about putting herself out there. Charisse always looked for love in all the wrong places, trying to fill some void she had because her father wasn't who she needed him to be. Although they were in the same house, he never paid her any attention until, as my mother observed, he had an itch that needed to be scratched. He treated her like Cinderella and her other siblings like they were more worthy than her. She was the product of his short marriage to her mother, his third wife who passed away from cirrhosis of the liver. He had very little to do with Charisse in terms of being a real father because he never wanted another child. She was to be seen but never heard.

He married Lois, Charisse's mother, for her money. He was a deadbeat with a fledgling junk business and his multiple marriages were really business deals to keep himself from going under. All of her life Charisse never saw her father treat any woman with respect and thus felt it was a fatal flaw to be a woman. Her remedy for this was to allow men to objectify her because she didn't know how else to be. No one ever showed her how to be a woman. No one ever showed her how to love herself and that she was more than something to be used, but her self-esteem would not allow her to believe that she did not need a man to affirm her existence.

I remember one night while I was still in high school, Charisse wound up on my doorstep in a bathrobe and slippers. On foot she was a good half hour walk from me. I recall her crumpling in the doorway like an accordion and breathing hard, the icy air billowing out of her mouth like liquid nitrogen. My mother was at the top of the stairs with a cigarette in hand and shaking her head.

"Somebody gonna kill that fool one day. Kill him dead! Aim and fire! That nigga ought to be shot. Sue, fix up the spare room....again," my mother said, stressing "again" due frustration over Charisse's inability to realize she did not have to take the abuse.

"What happened this time?

"He-he-he, he put the dog on me."

"Why that black..." my mother started.

"Ma!" I exclaimed.

"Ma nothing. What he do that for?"

"He, he, he was drinking and started on me about my mother and how she died, and she, and she left him no money."

"And so that's your fault? Uh huh, yeah. Sue Baby, load me up. We about to ride," my mother commanded while her cigarette flapped in the corner of her mouth between orders. At that moment she reminded me of those short-haired women I used to see when I was little. They didn't look too feminine and I wasn't sure why.

"Ma, don't get involved."

"I said we about to ride. Load me up!"

My mother was not about to back down. She had a rough night herself. She hit the number and sent the wrong person to pick up her money. She needed someone to drain her anger and put her in a better mood, and that was often achieved by getting in people's faces and brandishing a loaded gun, calling people black this and black that.

My mother was a fighter and a good one too. She didn't really look like one, but you saw it in her eyes. You knew she was slightly 'hood whenever she would answer the door in worn, pink, open-toed slippers, a thin bathrobe, and her short bob finger-combed back because she didn't wear a scarf to bed at times. Even on her worst day she was a pretty woman, but there was something behind her eyes that was darker than the dye in her hair. Too much hard living snuffed out their light.

"Baby girl, get your coat and leave your friend here. Charisse?"

"Yes m'am?" Charisse responded.

"Don't you set one foot out of this house. If I get to your Daddy's house... uh, excuse me, I mean your Daddy's fifteenth wife's house, and I see you beat me there, you and me got beef. We clear?"

She meant it. One thing my mother hated was to come to someone's rescue and then have them make a fool out of her by going back to the same thing again. Well, at least on the same night. Although I knew the ride was more about my mother and her anger more so than coming to Charisse's defense against her father, I was glad she was going to put the fear of god him.

"You got yours, Sue?" my mother asked, making sure I also had my unlicensed revolver loaded up and ready to shoot. I answered in the affirmative knowing full well the gun was laying at the bottom of the lake at the park. There was no way I was risking my chances of going to college following behind my mother and her rampages.

I tried to make an excuse to stay behind and my mind worked overtime to come up with one that would escape my mother's radar. She was street smart, and according to her self-assessment, more than slightly psychic. Oh, and psy*cho*. Sometimes she'd read palms and people would pay her. We had all kinds of stuff in the house to prove that she was serious about her abilities ranging from powders, dried chicken feet, and human hair.

I finally decided to speak up and put myself out of the misery of anticipating riding in the back of a patrol car over Charisse's father being a hooligan. I notified my mother that Charisse was too frightened to stay in the house by herself, and that she would be better off if I stayed behind to comfort her. That seemed to work.

A couple of hours had passed when my mother returned to the house with blood spattered on her shirt. Charisse let out a blood curdling scream, calling out for her father and asking god why did he take him from her. My mother just stood there, her eyes giving Charisse a "chile please", one hand on her hips, and the other in her pocket fumbling with something that made them bulge.

"Sue, shut that fool up! Nobody did nothing to that nut."

"What happened then? You have blood on your shirt," I asked.

"Let's just say he can close his Pet World account," my mother said as she pulled her hand out of her pocket to reveal a few five's and one's. No doubt it was money from Charisse's father. Knowing my mother, she probably made him pay her for getting blood on her shirt and burning gas to go over there to shoot the dog.

That memory made me think about my mother and men in general, how she was always in control and never allowed any of them to disrespect her. I was her only child, the product of the only man she had who was worth anything but she couldn't see it. She taught me that men were worthless, but I knew it was because she chose the wrong ones. She preferred the numbers runners, the drug dealers—the ones who could teach her how to shoot guns or how to hit someone in the throat to end a fight before it started. My mother would always tell me a man was only good for one thing and whatever else I needed I was to get it myself. I learned that if a man ever thought a woman depended on him, he would lose respect for her, use her, and take his business elsewhere when he was done. In her mind love meant nothing because it wasn't real. She was a soldier of love, taking no prisoners and only leaving casualties. Unfortunately, I was one but didn't know it.

I was doing alright minding my business until one of the guys laughed out loud and gave his boys a high five yelling, "Cherry about to go pop!" And I wish I knew what made me do it, but I couldn't say. Maybe it was my ego that drove me because, even though I didn't feel like defending my friend, the fact that this guy was continuing to talk about her within earshot knowing I was her friend was, in my mind, even more disrespectful than what he was alluding to. Maybe it was because I was too deep in thought over my past and my mother's gun-toting rampage that, although my body was back, my mind and emotions were still a few years away. The bottom line was that I was still a little tipsy and didn't think about the repercussions for showing that loud mouth who was boss before I marched back up to Naziir's room. The only thing I remember from that moment was someone gasping for air and holding his throat. I don't even remember if I stopped at one person. In a blind rage, I dug in the garbage can to find a glass bottle to take with me to the room. I didn't have time to go outside and break it at the bottom. With weapon in hand, I was so anxious to remedy whatever darkness was happening a few floors above me that I couldn't wait for the elevator. I took the stairs and each step felt like a stairway to hell. The color red paid me another visit, but in a hue more crimson than the one that painted me earlier that day.

I didn't even know why I was so upset because Charisse's behavior was no surprise to me. Maybe I needed an excuse to be mad about something and my anger in that situation was warranted. I was just mad. Mad at jesus for coming down from the cloud and knocking me down, mad at Mari for talking instead of listening, and fuming at Delilah for crossing my path with her fake happiness like life was good all the time. I wondered what she would do if she were in my situation. Would she jab someone in the throat? Would she march up to some guy's room to rescue her friend? Probably not and that made me madder. By the time I reached the fifth floor, I wasn't sure what my motive was anymore. I just knew I had a bad feeling and was suddenly reminded of the dream I had with Charisse dancing in the red dress and the initial "V" on the handkerchief. I had to get up to that room.

As I stopped for a moment to catch my breath, I overheard shuffling in the room and a small voice that sounded muffled like someone's hand was over its mouth. I looked at the bottom of the door and saw the reflection in the floor of a dim, flickering light. Candles. I knew something was up. Who plays cards in the dark?

"Yo! Open this door!" I yelled, banging and kicking at room 515 like there was a fire inside. "Yo! Naziir! I said open this door! Charisse!"

I kept kicking and screaming and banging until rooms 513, 509, and 500 came out to see what the commotion was.

"Can't you people ever have a kumbaya moment?"

"Take that back to the 'hood, Shaniqua!"

"What do you mean by *you people*? Who you calling Shaniqua? You mind your business!" I retorted.

"Yo' mama, homie!"

"Dude, no really, you just took your life in your hands with that one!"

"Well she can call the NAACP."

My head was spinning. It was spinning so fast that it came off its axis and spun into someone else's orbit. I was spinning and spinning, way past Earth, past Mars, and past Venus. It finally made its way to the closest planet to the Sun, Mercury.    And it was hot. So hot that when one of the other planets in the room—probably Pluto—tried to pull me away from the door, I grabbed all the rings from Saturn and began hurling them in every direction like frisbees. The hallway was on its way to becoming a super nova when I was finally stopped by the gravitational pull of the moon. The door swung open and Vince peeked his head outside.

"Uh, what are you doing?"

I ignored him and called for Charisse.

"Your girl is, um, busy," Vince announced to me and rooms 513, 509, and 500.

I kept calling for Charisse, threatening to tell my mother she was about to make a fool out of her child.

"Vince, let me by," Charisse said while buttoning up her blouse and fixing her hair. "My friend is tripping and she will not leave unless I come out."

Vince looked me up and down and sucked his teeth, calling me a jealous robot.

"What is wrong with you?" Charisse asked, staring at me and shaking her head like I was the one with the problem. I didn't answer her. I had her by the arm and wouldn't let her go until we got to her room, 808.

"You can go now," Charisse said. I had no intentions of leaving. "You know you embarrassed me up there. I can make my own decisions. I'm grown."

I was still silent, half angry at Charisse for being a fool and angry at myself for not being able to fully justify why I was really feeling the way I was. I just knew I had enough of whatever was eating away at me.

"Take a shower, please. You smell like a bottom feeder fish."

"You are so rude! You get on my nerves acting like you're my mother!"

"You weren't saying that all those times you came to my house in the middle of the night running from your father!"

In between shouts there was a knock at the door. It was the campus police. I was shocked because I wasn't exactly sure of all I had done.

"Young lady, come with us."

I couldn't believe it. I spent my entire academic career trying not to get arrested for doing what I was taught to do all of my life. It was two months before graduation and I was about to take a different kind of photo.

When the police escorted me outside, we passed where I bumped into Delilah earlier that day. As I hung my head in shame, my eyes noticed one of the bible tracts that was missed in my effort to help Delilah pick up the ones I knocked out of her bag. Something warm overtook my body as I thought how strange it was that my day seemed to come full circle.

Right before I was placed in the back of the patrol car, I took a look at the sky. The moon was as full as ever, and I saw a small cloud slowly pass in front of it and it looked down at me with a look of concern. I felt like it was summoned on my behalf. The jesus cloud was back.

"Er, um, come again?"

"M'am, your daughter has been taken into custody for assault and battery with a weapon, and for disturbing the peace," the sergeant explained to my mother.

"Has she been charged?"

"No m'am. We are talking with the victim now to see if he wants to proceed."

"He???" my mother said in disbelief, stressing the "h" to give the "s" time to find its rightful place in front of it. But she was to be disappointed. "You tell that pink pansy he ain't no man letting a girl whoop on him. And he is less than a lesser man if he presses charges! And what, pray tell, was the weapon? A feather?"

I could see the officer's frustration as he sparred back and forth with my mother while attempting to get her to understand that her opinion of the guy, and his inability to defend himself against two projectile objects—one human and one inanimate—was irrelevant. Her daughter might be going to jail right before graduation.

"Y'all doing this because she's black! If she was a white girl you'd call it a beer pong induced cat fight and send her back to the dorms in a limousine! Racists!"

"M'am, this is not about race. It's about your daughter..."

"Racists!"

"M'am..."

"And how do you know she did it? Cause somebody that looks like you said so?"

"M'am, we have witnesses."

"And who are those witnesses? Other people that look like you?"

The officer's face balled up in further frustration and he seemed as though he wanted to answer my mother's question with a "No, there were some people there who looked like you too!", but he didn't say it. The so-called racist officer had a picture of his family on his desk, all of them bunched together looking like Neapolitan ice cream. He was vanilla, his wife was chocolate and the kids were strawberry.

While I was trying to concentrate on the officer's conversation with my mother, I was distracted by two other officers talking in low tones and putting a thumb tack in a photo. All I could hear was how two more women came in complaining about some disease and how the police could no longer ignore what was going on. Finally the officer was off the phone with my mother. Wiping the sweat from his forehead, he looked at me with an exasperated look as though he were asking me how in the world do I do it.

"Young lady, off the record, may I ask what possessed you to do what you did?"

I didn't even remember what I did. I proceeded to tell him all I could remember. He looked puzzled when I began to talk about the solar system, but his face returned to normal when I said I was trying to save my friend from something bad happening and some people got in my way.

"So let me get this straight. You broke a bottle over someone's head for calling you Shaniqua?" the officer asked while shaking his head.

"Officer," I replied. "I felt threatened. All these guys in the hallway and just one of me."

"I would buy your argument except for the fact that witnesses said you already had the bottle in your hand. Now I'm going to assume you found it at the moment when all the action took place. Am I assuming correctly? Because if not, that would indicate premeditation. Do you understand me?"

"Yes sir."

"I'm going to talk to the boy you clobbered and see if he still wants to press charges. In the meantime, you sit here and think about how you more than likely ruined your chances of graduating from this university, no matter if you are charged or not."

If there was ever a time I needed to pray, it was then. I never even thought about prayer outside of hoping for something and crossing my fingers, but there is something about being found in a jam that would make the unreligious religious. *Very* religious.

I thought about the bible tract Delilah gave me and pulled it out of my pocket. Maybe there was something in there like a chant or something that I could repeat over and over to turn things around. My mother did so whenever she was in trouble. She had these rituals she learned from my grandmother where she would tie a white scarf on her head, burn candles, and smear that green paste on the doorposts of every room in the house. She even learned about having parties in the basement from my grandmother. She'd dress up a long banquet table with fruit, candy, and other stuff. She said it was for some spirits to make them happy and work on her behalf. Every time she had those parties, the candy and food would be gone, yet no one claimed to have eaten them and there was never any trash.

I never believed in whatever power my mother claimed to call on, but she would tell me stories that would freak me out and make me want to believe in something in order to protect me. When I calmed down, I realized it was probably too much beer or a laced cigarette that made her hallucinate, but my mother swears the things she felt and saw were real.

"Suzi, there may not be some supreme god up above, but let me tell you, there are forces in this world. There's good ones and bad ones. You plug into the right one, you can harness both. Let me tell you a story."

My mother would usually tell me her personal horror stories at night while in the kitchen greasing my scalp with some special ointment from a tin can. She would take a black rat tail comb and part my hair with the tail while scratching my scalp with the "rat". In between scratches, she would stop and remark how she got a "big one" and parted my hair even more carefully to make sure she didn't disturb it. For some reason she got great joy out of lifting up big pieces of dead skin. Afterwards, she would take a boar's bristle brush and sweep out the flakes that were caught in my hair. Sometimes I noticed her putting my shed hair and flakes of dandruff in a small bag, but I never asked why she did that.

Even though I never put much credence in my mother's stories, one she told me in particular burned in my mind. She told me as a teenager my grandmother would take her to church and she'd watch her do what they called "sopping". This was where they would put themselves in the presence of people who were believed to be spiritually gifted. My grandmother would pretend to need prayer or hands laid on her. When they touched hands, while the christian would pray, my grandmother would also pray, but not to jesus. She would pray to whatever spirit she harnessed to sop all the strength and supernatural gifts from the christian. She said she was only able to do it when the person was puffed up in pride and felt it was no longer necessary to pray and fast. All the false praise and accolades made them feel they had spiritually arrived.

My grandmother said something about in the christian religion, the only way a gift would work was if the person was truly living for their god. If not, the gift was up for grabs. Any spirit could use it or take it and give it to somebody else. And if you wanted it, all you had to do was touch them and not just physically, but also mentally by making them think they were the only ones who could help you. That would make the pride in them swell and dull whatever sense they had to alert them that they were being sopped.

After my grandmother would get the gift she needed, she would take a bath with rosewater and oil then call people on the phone and tell them their future. It would last for a week, then she would travel to another church and do the same thing again. People called her a church hopper, but they didn't know she hopped to sop.

"But one night, I declare Suzi Baby god rest your grandmamma soul, I think she sopped from the wrong one because that very night I heard her hollering and running and screaming and repeating some scripture all night about not touching god's anointed and doing them no harm. When I ran in the room to see what the racket was, I saw her hanging from the ceiling by her feet. Girl, her feet! I mean there was no rope, no wire, no nothing! Looking like somebody was shaking the change out of her pockets except no coins was hitting the ground. And the bible was underneath her and flipping itself back and forth and stopping on that scripture she was reciting. I said, 'Mama how you get up there?' and she said in a man's voice, 'Run, Esther! Run outta here! This here is between me and the christian god!' So I ran, but when I looked back something ran past me and all I saw was a tail split in two and pointing in opposite directions. One was pointing  north and the other was pointing way down south. After it was all over, your grandmamma said that thing with the tail was the dirty laundry. That happens when you sop from a sopper."

Thinking about the story made me want to read the bible tract all the more and tell my mother to stop getting high. Besides that, I was full of fear about my future, my mother possibly using me for target practice when I finally returned home, and fear that I would lose my best friend because she wouldn't be caught dead with a jailbird. The fear of known and unknown consequences caused me to do the inevitable. I read the tract from the beginning, rereading the passage about the wind, then continuing to read about the power of the holy spirit to convict people of sin and help renew the mind as the path to a new life. It read that the holy spirit would reveal and exalt jesus christ in the life of a person who believed, and was also a comforter. I needed to be comforted, and as much as I hated to admit, those words were right on time.

In my desperation I prayed a short prayer and made a pact with god that if he got me out of that jam I would go to the seven o'clock bible study, and maybe even church on Sunday. I would stop acting foolish and be calm. I asked him to give me a sign if he heard me. I was still in eternity when the officer came back with my verdict.

"Looks like the plot is thickening as we speak. More witnesses came forward and are giving a different side of the story. Supposedly one of the boys in the hall grabbed the bottle from you and the force of it made him swing into his friend."

Although I didn't fully remember, one side of me was saying, "Yeah, that's what happened" and the other part of me was disappointed in not getting credit for putting someone to sleep.

"I'm inclined to believe these witnesses only because they have no reason to lie. Matter of fact, they'd rather get hit in the head with two bottles before they tell a tale. So this is what I'm going to do for you. I will release you on your own recognizance, but you will have to go before the university about your conduct. Whether you started, finished, or in-betweened it, you will have to answer for your conduct."

"jesus!" I yelled out involuntarily. When I realized it left my mouth, I covered it with both hands. I didn't want to appear like those jesus people on campus.

After my mother was called and she gave the officer another ear full, I thought about going back to Charisse's room to go off on her about what happened. It was because of her I had a bad feeling in the first place, which despite all that happened, was still present. But then I thought about my brand new pact with god and how it just might not be a coincidence that someone spoke up for me and not against me.

As I walked outside in the wee hours of the morning, I saw a small crowd of three talking who looked like they would go into the mountains and drink poison because god told them to. "Uh" and "oh" collided on my tongue when I realized I was looking at Shadrach, Meshach and ThereDelilahGo.

"We just couldn't let them lie on you," Delilah confessed. "We saw the whole thing. We were having all night prayer and heard what was going on and…"

Delilah continued by saying one of her christian friends looked to see what the commotion was at the point one of the guys grabbed the bottle from me because I was swinging it like crazy by its neck. They must have figured it was a matter of time before it would fly out of my hand. When the one who confiscated it accidentally hit his friend and saw I was still out of sorts and didn't notice, the christians overheard the guys plotting to say it was me. Delilah saved the best part of the story for last. The officer who arrested and questioned me was the uncle of one of her prayer partners. That's why he believed them so readily. That was all the sign I needed.

"Delilah, I'm ready to go to bible study. I will see you there tonight."

"Praise be to God! Hosanna in the highest!!!"

I didn't want too much attention on what I said, but my mind and body were so tired and exasperated from the day into morning that I had to give in. However, a little part of me had enough energy to inquire about what exactly was the conversation they had while they were all huddled together. It seemed like it was just about more than me as I heard whispers.

"When I came out and you all were talking and shaking your heads, were you talking about me?"

"No," Delilah answered. "Actually, we were talking about the guy the police are looking for. Supposedly there's this guy on campus who is HIV positive and has been fornicating without telling people his status. Ten girls from three different campuses went to the police. Two more came forward tonight."

"What's his name? You know?"

"Um, let me see," Delilah pondered as she turned to her friend.

"Hey Chuck, do you remember the guy's name the police are looking for?"

"I don't know," Chuck answered. "But according to my uncle, they are looking for him right now. That might be them coming this way."

Slow motion was not the word to describe how my body moved as I turned around to see who was coming towards us. My body felt as though all the blood was being drained the closer the police came with the person in custody. As they passed us, the suspect looked my way and all I could see and feel was death. That death had a name; it was Vince.

The first thought that came to my mind was how I kept getting a bad feeling when we went to play cards. My protective instincts kicked in without even knowing that there was imminent danger. I even heard the usual *bang* whenever something was going on with Charisse, but I had no idea it would mean her life. The words of Federline haunted me as I remembered the night he said Charisse's dress was red as blood, and also the dream I had the night before we left for college. I vividly recalled the flames that licked up her body and the monogrammed handkerchief that the beast in the dream had in its pocket. The "V" didn't just stand for Vince; it stood for H.I.V. My friend was going to die over a game of cards and a beer, and I was going to die from accepting the fact that I had a premonition that came to pass to the letter. That was not something my science textbooks could explain. It was time for my denial to stop.

I was exhausted from thinking and I slept so hard that I felt trapped in a nightmare and wanted to die in it. Madame Samedie came to me, but instead of walking towards me, she stood in one place and yelled at me from afar. She beckoned me to come to her, but I first had to tell her "yes" because someone was interfering with my permission. If I did not say so, she said I would become a curse and kill my mother. Before I could purse my lips together to answer in the affirmative, the thing or person that always jumped between us whenever I dreamt about her as a child became clearly visible. It was a lady dressed in white and she wielded a sword that had the number seven engraved in different fonts and sizes. She twisted the sword with one hand, turned around with the force of a tornado, and beheaded Madam Samedie. Instead of blood gushing everywhere, a black viscous liquid slowly oozed out of her neck. The four heads appeared, just like in the ceremony, and one by one each drowned in the liquid.

"Schizophrenia!" the lady called out. "The Lord rebuke you!"

"Who are you?" I asked in the dream. "Who are you?"

"I'm your intercessor," the woman said. "And do you know who you are?

"I'm Suzi, Esther's child."

"No! You're Suzi, God's child! You're ready. Let's go!"

When she said "Let's go", I bolted out of my dream and threw my hands in the air as though something was leaving my body that I had to catch and put back inside of me. It kept floating away from me, and it floated up to the ceiling then came back down and landed right beside me. It looked at me and I looked at it, and then I realized that I was staring at myself but with four heads. I screamed but the other me did not scream with me. It rolled over and tried to fit itself back into my body, the heads knocking against each other like Ka Bangers going at warp speed, but it could not fit. I screamed for everyone I knew and didn't know. I even screamed for god, and I saw one of the heads disappear. I then screamed for Delilah, and the remaining heads looked slightly nervous then shook it off. I finally wore myself down to call for jesus, and that was when each head opened its mouth and swallowed the one in front of it. The last one attempted to swallow me. I could smell the stale syrup that was the Monster Me's saliva. And before I gagged, I had the strength to repeat what I heard the intercessor say in the dream, "Schizophrenia, the Lord rebuke you!" At that moment I felt a warm sensation as though something was blanketing me with protection.

It took a long time before I was able to get out of bed. I took inventory of all that happened and began to daydream to return to my version of normal. I went through all the motions by shooting people for the same reasons, then jerked, and still didn't die. I was to live another day in and out of my head.

I began to think about how I was going to break it to Charisse that her one night of passion might lead her to the grave. I couldn't bear the thought of being the bearer of bad news because of all the things she had gone through all of her life. Her mother passed away, her father was a drunken fool, and it was my fault I left her in the room. It was my fault for taking the time to hit The Gabber in the throat instead of immediately marching up to Naziir's room as soon as I heard Cherry was about to go pop. Instead, I wasted time being a bully and in those split seconds might have killed my friend. But then maybe she didn't go all the way with Vince but instead they may have just rubbed legs and made cricket sounds.

I didn't realize through all of the commotion that Mari was nowhere to be found. I was sure at some point someone must have told her what happened, but no phone call, no visit, no nothing. She was not used to so much drama because she came from a more stable environment, and while her life was not perfect, she managed to give the illusion that it was. Although we had a lot in common, there was a lot we didn't have in common. The thing that brought us together was that we provided an escape for each other, but at some point I began to feel that I was doing most of the escaping while she transitioned into tolerating. Our interdependent relationship became one of dependence and I could clearly see the scales weighed heavily on Mari's side.

I remember the first day we met when she transferred to my junior high school from some private school in Manhattan. Her parents were experiencing financial difficulty and had to put her in public school. Because she was pretty and decently off by my neighborhood's standards, a lot of people made assumptions about what she thought of herself. I, on the other hand, never cared about what a person wore or what they looked like. My family had money all the time. It wasn't always clean money, but it was money nonetheless. I wasn't impressed with anything Mari had because, knowing my mother, she would buy me two of everything if I wanted. The only thing I lacked was someone who would talk to me on my level and listen to me, and not have me always listen to them. I needed someone I could be weak around when I didn't feel like being strong, and Mari showed her strength from the start.

"So you're new here?" I asked Mari as she seemed to fish for a friendly spot in the junior high cafeteria. "You can sit with me and my friend Charisse. We know you're cool."

"Thank you, but I don't need a bodyguard. I can handle myself," Mari replied trying to show she wasn't afraid.

"Well, I heard you went to school in Manhattan and all, but out here on the Island we can scrap, too. You may as well make friends fast before someone tries to test you in here. People already aren't feeling you."

"What is this? Prison? Some kind of gang initiation? Do I need to be jumped in or something? I said I got it."

"Girl, what you got is a tray of hot food getting cold because you have nowhere to sit! Those taters are tottin'!"

We both couldn't help but laugh because Mari knew she was hungry and had to sit down. Unfortunately, Charisse was not too happy that I was on the verge of making a new friend. And even though after some time we all were considered a trio, I knew Charisse secretly hated Mari for many reasons— reasons she would never let go of and reasons which Mari was aware but didn't care enough to address. As far as Mari was concerned, I was the outfit and Charisse was the handbag she may or may not carry that day.

I decided not to waste any more time and just tell Charisse what happened. The longer I waited, the more I would torture myself with what ifs. But, I had to call my mother first. The phone had been ringing off the hook since I returned from the station, but I didn't want to answer it. I was in no mood for my mother's rant. And "whomever was in the sky" forbid if she had a sip of something before she called. I took a deep breath and prepared myself to ask my mother if she wanted me on wheat or white.

"You know what, girl child? I'm not even mad at you on one level."

I couldn't believe it and I sure didn't trust it. My mother proceeded to tell me a story to explain why she was not that mad. She was inclined to give me a pass because of her racial prejudice despite being part white herself. Thinking about my maternal lineage felt like one big run-on because my great grandmother was an octoroon who had my grandmother by a mulatto, which made her a quadroon, I guess, so my mother was not quite mulatto but not quite white or black, so she called herself a quintlatto if there's such a thing, which in my eyes still made me black thanks to my father who was what my mother would call a "pot bottom". She only dated dark-skinned men because she wanted her child to be caramel colored, or darker, with thick wavy hair that was not too coarse and not too straight. However, if she got mad with someone she was the first to call them out by their color from one end of the spectrum to the other: clear; ivory; red bone; high yella; light bright; pecan tan; walnut shell; paper bag; cream soda; wax paper; summer season brown; caramel; Snicker bar; maple syrup; ebony; and night time.

Her irrational feelings about race came from her desire to escape bad family history because of a contract one of the greats in the family, Lady Mae, signed in order to obtain her freedom from slavery. She had a so-called benevolent slave master who no longer wanted to run his plantation but rather move to Europe to try his fortune in trading. He sold all of his slaves except for Lady Mae, who was his house slave and paramour. He couldn't bring her with him to Europe because of his wife, but he didn't want to sell her because he knew what she would suffer at the hands of another slave master who would most likely not be very humane towards his slaves. Lady Mae begged him to grant her freedom, but it came at a price.

"He made Lady Mae sign a contract that if he let her go she was to remain pure, as in she was to never sleep with a black man. That went for all first-born girl children for four generations. He got some conjure woman to seal it with Lady Mae's blood and spittle. By the time the curse of the contract got to the last one, your grandmamma, well, you know she was a sopper and she wasn't afraid of nobody's curses. She didn't go too black, though. She got with a half-black man, your granddaddy. When I was born the curse was lifted, so me being wild and free got the blackest thing I could find. You know your daddy is jet black. He's so black that when he went to West Virginia to work in the coal mines, he would always come back with all kinds of nicks in his skin because the other miners would accidentally shovel his blasted soul!"

And with that she let out a laugh so hard that I could hear her slapping her knee and knocking over something. She apologized claiming she knocked over her stick pins, burlap, wax, and feathers—materials she gathered in case I was held too long at the police station and needed some supernatural help.

"So I'm not mad at ya, honey. That fight was in Lady Mae's honor. Well done."

Even though I was relieved that my mother was not upset with me, I was slightly disturbed that she didn't mention her feelings about me possibly not graduating.

"I might be taking my life in my hands here, but you know this could get me kicked out of school," I explained.

My mother paused for a second before she responded.

"Girl child, you made me proud all of your life. I will allow you this one mistake. And you will graduate from college, so help me. Maybe not where you at now, but from somewhere. Don't you worry."

I couldn't believe my ears. Even though my mother was a firecracker—and even smoked a few—I knew that she cared. She was often in her own world and left me to be in mine, but in her special way she would reveal the gem in her heart. While she was in her tender moment, I thought to bring up Charisse.

"Honey, you ain't telling me nothing I ain't already figured would happen. That girl is a tragedy. Surprised it took this long."

"So how do I tell her?" I asked, hoping she would volunteer.

"Tell her."

Simple as that. Just tell her. I still didn't know how and I certainly didn't want to go back to her dorm to possibly face my accusers and have the same thing happen all over again. I thought maybe I should call her, but that was not something to tell someone over the phone. I'd call her over, but after the way I spoke to her that night, she wouldn't want to be bothered. I decided to just pick up the phone.

"Hello, Charisse?"

Before I had a chance to say anything more, she had already hung up the phone. I called back but she refused to pick up. I resorted to calling my mother and have her tell Charisse to call me. That did the trick because Charisse knew not to get on my mother's bad side.

"Your mother said to call you and that's the *only* reason I'm calling you," Charisse said dryly.

I proceeded to tell her about my trip to the station, how I was lied on, then my mother told the officer off, then I noticed two girls coming in, two cops coming in with a guy, Vince, and I'm so sorry.

"You are such a liar!!!" Charisse screamed while enunciating every single syllable. The victim was about to come out in 3-2-1. "You don't want me to have anything! Nobody does! Not even my own father!"

"Why would I lie about something like that?" I asked.

"Because you're mean! Always telling me what to do, always acting like my mother, always serious and stiff about everything!"

"Always bailing you out of a jam, always fighting for you, always letting you be the victim, always always always! You're not in this mess because I'm so mean or because I act like your mother. You're in this mess because of you! Own it!"

I hung up the phone so hard that the world covered its ears. I had enough on my plate wondering if I would get kicked out of school or not, dealing with my anger issues that seemed to stem from nothing and something at the same time, angry over Mari not even calling to check on me, mad about the promise I made to Delilah to go to bible study on a Friday night...just mad! And before I knew it, I was in a field of burnt grass with iron ore all over the place. There was a man standing in the center of the field who called himself The Blacksmith. He asked me what did I want him to fashion for me, so I asked for a gun. He said if I wanted a gun I'd have to daydream further into the future because I was back in medieval times. So I settled for a sword and shield. He said he would make them but they might be too heavy for me to handle. So I asked why was he asking me what I wanted if everything I asked for he couldn't make? He said he'd make me a knife. I asked him what could I do with that? He said I could use it to cut the cancer out of my life. "What cancer?" I asked. He said, "You."

I was jolted out of my "daymare" by a knock on my door. If it was Delilah picking me up hours early for bible study, I was going to go back to The Blacksmith and put in an order. To my surprise it was Mari. My eyes lit up as she walked in the room, but she barely wanted to look at me. She looked heavy as though she were buckling under the weight of our friendship, one that seemed more like a figment of my imagination than an actual one.

"I heard what happened," Mari informed me.

"So where were you? You were M.I.A. all this time? When did you find out?"

"That's not important. Look Suzi, we've been friends for a long time and you know I love you like a sister, but this is really the last straw."

*So that was the burning grass.*

"What do you mean last straw? I don't get it," I said while showing my confusion.

"Suzi, we are about to graduate and I have plans for grad school. I want to get involved with some organizations, you know, progressive things and, well, I'm just going to say it. The way you live your life right now just doesn't fit with where I'm trying to go."

*So that was the knife.*

I sat down on my bed with my eyes hitting the ground in hopes of finding a better explanation somewhere. Possibly there was one that was accidentally swept under the rug, a chair, the desk, or somewhere. I couldn't find it.

"So let me get this straight," I started. "Do you mean to tell me that in order to be your friend I have to be perfect?"

"I'm telling you that this anger problem you have is killing our friendship. You're just too angry nowadays and I don't know what's gotten into you. You won't seek help and when a person doesn't want to help herself, that's when it's time to bail out."

*So that's the cancer.*

Mari continued her assassination of my imperfections, leading me to believe that our whole friendship had been a farce. As long as I didn't interfere with her ability to get in good with the right people, she was okay. The minute it was known to the world that she had a friend with flaws, she had to hide me and hide me good. Surely I held her back from her goals. Surely I did so although we were getting the same education and had the same core values. Clearly it was an outside job.

"Who put you up to this?" I asked with certainty that my curiosity would be satisfied.

"No one put me up to this. I mean, Suzi…"

"It was your mother, wasn't it? You called and told her what happened and she told you to do what she's been waiting for all along."

As tight as Mari and I were, her mother never warmed up to me. Her dislike of me was furthered by who my mother was and wasn't because I lived in a household with no permanent males, and on special occasions we didn't eat on fine china. The whole neighborhood knew my mother read palms and shook bones in a bag, and that my house was the house where there was always someone standing in the window even when no one was home. Mari's mother constantly warned her to stay away from me because she believed my mother was a witch and did all kinds of voodoo.

Mari confirmed that although she did tell her mother what happened with me and the police, the decision she made to end our friendship was a long time coming. She confessed that the closeness we had was more on my end than hers. She knew I needed the stability her parents gave, but she was at the point in her life where she was no longer in the mood to give emotional handouts. We were not kids anymore but young women with hopes and dreams that often hinged on the favor of people who expect us to fit into a certain mold. For Mari, it was time for mutual friendship with people of her background and on her level, whatever it was. She was upward bound and could not afford to ruin her reputation with the circles she desired to get into on the count of me. It was hard to swallow that our friendship had an expiration date: I/Ambetterthanyou/1993. I knew it wasn't Mari talking. I could smell the stench of her mother's influence so strongly that I held my nose in defiance and screamed, "You and your mother's words, the both of you get out!" and slammed the door behind my longtime friend. And with that I was two for two losing friends. I was about to be three for three, the third being my mind. I truly felt all by myself and planned to wallow in a briny sea of tears and cry myself to sleep when the phone rang. It was my mother again.

"Girl you WHAT?!" she screamed.

"What are you talking about?" I asked, startled at her tone of voice after such a heartwarming conversation earlier. Well, heartwarming by her standards.

"You about to get kicked out of school. You about to waste my money up in that camp acting a straight fool!"

"Ma," I protested. "I thought you weren't upset about it!"

"Girl, I was high. I'm down now. Way down and ready to cock it back and start squeezing!"

I held the phone away from my ear as my mother ranted and raved and demanded that I get my mind right and get it in perspective. When I brought up my contribution to Lady Mae's memory, she said Lady Mae had been dead for over a century and what about that old biddy anyway? By the time she finished I felt hurt, betrayed, angry, and alone. I didn't have an ounce of trust in anyone I held dear because in one day everyone flipped on me and I just about had enough. By the time I allowed myself to cry, it was nearing 7 o'clock and I knew I had to put up or shut up with the church thing. Whether it was fake or not, I needed a dose of that happiness Delilah seemed to always have, even if it appeared plastered on. It was either that or some kind of death, and at that moment any death would do.

Before I knew it I was standing in front of the christian Student Center watching a herd gathering and talking excited, loud, and fast. Everyone seemed so happy and eager to engage in that night's bible study. I was still angry and hurt towards Delilah for having come into my space and making me deal with something I realized I probably wasn't ready to. I remember before I left for college that my mother warned me about christian groups on campus. She said they grab college kids and brainwash them, then have them running around all day trying to change people who didn't want to be changed. In her estimation, church was designed to draw impressionable people who were either too early in their lives to have an identity, or at a point where they felt their options had run out and so why not give somebody's god a try. She said if she were god she'd reject those people because their belief and allegiance were only need-based.

My mother also claimed that my grandmother rejected organized religion after a certain incident, which she never revealed to her. My father's side attended church, although they were not what you would call fanatics. When my parents were together, my father almost got my mother to go to church for the right reasons more than once. But when she found out the reverend was tipping out on his wife and every youth that walked through the door looked like him, she knew it was not for her. Besides, my grandmother was a sopper who claimed she got results and saw things in the future without ever calling on anybody's god. All of that talk of living right and not sitting in the seat of the scornful in order to get close to god and have all of your prayers answered was, in my mother's words, "Just a cool drink on a hot day for the desperate masses. And if the day ever came when their thirst stopped being quenched, they would just find another cup to drink from."

The moment of truth—somebody's truth—had come. The doors opened and my feet were moving on their own. I didn't see Delilah and I kind of didn't want to see her, but as the jesus cloud would have it, she would eventually find me and stick to me like glue the whole time. I sat in the back so I could run out when I didn't feel quite right. I pretty much expected at some point that I would be turned off, run out, my world would return to normal, and everything would be okay. But then the fallouts that occurred earlier reminded me that things would not be alright unless something changed.

As I sat in the back watching everyone, I looked around the room at all of the words and symbols on the wall. On one wall it looked like the silhouette of a dove and the word "Pneuma" was written underneath it. Then directly opposite the dove was a silhouette of a man with long hair and outstretched arms. Underneath him was the word "Logos". In the center of the church were just clouds and rays shooting from them with the word "Father" written inside the clouds. When I saw those words my heart ached. That's what I needed at that moment; someone to lift me up into the clouds and love me like a father would love his child. I needed heart protection, which I felt was not offered to me enough.

I continued to survey the room and noticed a crest on the pulpit. It had a knight's mask and two swords on either side of a shield. The swords reminded me of The Blacksmith who was at that point out of my head and seated behind me with a knife in my back. I wasn't sure if it was mine or not, and I wasn't sure if he had planned to stab me or use it to cut the cancer out. I decided to ask.

"Well said. I am about to cut the cancer out because you cannot do it alone."

"But why from behind?" I asked.

"Because you cannot handle seeing the root."

"What does it look like?"

"You."

By the time The Blacksmith said "You", I was jolted back into reality and realized the bible study leader was already teaching and had emphasized the word "You" to the congregation.

"Many of us don't want to admit it, but our worst enemy is one of the greatest sabotagers of all time. That enemy is often *you*."

He went on to talk about how we make the wrong choices in life, come from families who do not instill the right values, and embrace philosophies that divide rather than unite. He explained how many people sitting in the room were hurting and holding on to it so long that it had taken root as bitterness. He used the bible to point out examples of the christian god's love and how as a christian, it is commanded to love people who are our neighbors and also our enemies.

"The Bible says when your mother and father forsake you, the Lord will take you up. And let me take that a step further. When your friends forsake you, there is a man who sticks closer to you than a brother. His name is Jesus and he is the one who can stop that cancer in your body from growing. He can cut the cancer out of you by that two-edged sword, the Word of God, through the power of the Holy Spirit!"

Despite my best efforts to hold back my tears, they rolled down my face one by one, and each tear recited an elegy for each other before reaching my chin and committing suicide by plunging into the abyss of whatever I could find to catch their desperate, pear-shaped bodies. The sleeve of my blouse would become a makeshift morgue for all the tears that represented my hurt, my pain, my disappointments, the things I felt that I couldn't understand, and all of the above. I was confused because I had a hole in my heart and didn't know how it got there. Why wasn't I alright?

I began to think long and hard about where my problem with my anger began. I was never hungry, never cold, never naked, and never alone. But I did often feel "different" in the sense that my family was not like everyone else's. Different in that I had to learn how to not let the stares, the snickering, the gossip, all the uncles, and scary stories floating around in the neighborhood about the women in my family get to me.

I spent a good deal of my life ignoring what was around me in order to stay sane. As long as I was clothed and fed, I thought everything was good. I would lock myself in my room and dream—sometimes about something and other times about nothing. But any dream was better than some of the harsh realities I used to think were normal until I began hanging around Mari. She pointed out to me that some of the normalities in my home weren't normal at all. She was the one to convince me to lock my room door whenever a new uncle came to visit, and put a little drop of some olive oil from a tiny vial on my forehead, which was a little something her father brought home from church that was prayed over. She said it was holy oil and it would protect me from that thing the neighbors always said looked out my window when no one was home. Even though I never saw what they were talking about, I put the oil on my head anyway out of respect for Mari. I never wanted to lie to her and say I did something I didn't do.

The first time I ever visited Mari's house I remember feeling uncomfortable. It wasn't because her parents always looked at me as though I had two heads, or even that I knew somehow that her mother truly didn't like me as a friend for her. There was just something in the air that didn't sit right with me. When more of her family was around, the discomfort grew stronger. Mari's high school graduation party was the time I finally couldn't take it anymore, and I ran into the bathroom and stayed there to try to figure out why, on such a happy occasion, I was red hot.

"Suzi, you in there?" Mari called. I knew her question was rhetorical, yet I muffled out a weak affirmation and pulled my knees up to my chin even more.

"Come on out," she said quietly. "There's no one in the house except us. Everyone's outside."

I didn't want to come out, partly because I was embarrassed that I took the attention away from her special moment and didn't know why. She had the answer.

"Suzi, every time my family comes around you shut down. Every other time you are bold as a lion, but when you come here you crawl into this shell."

"Why do I feel like this?" I asked in between snots.

"Suzi, you don't know how to handle being around stability. That's what it is."

And she was right. There was always turmoil lurking in my life and in my home. Someone was always fighting, always talking about shooting someone, always shaking a chicken foot and collecting spider webs to do somebody something. And every now and then there'd be some drug dealer pimp type from as far as The Bronx dating my mother who smelled like heavy cologne and 8 karat rose gold.

"I knew he wasn't right. What kinda man wears rose gold?" my mother said after breaking up with the last man she ever brought home, her gun still smoking from the several shots she fired at him for trying to get into my room while she was asleep. It was locked because I took Mari's advice. If I believed in it, I would say she had a premonition.

"I dare you today to take a leap of faith and join me at this altar," the bible study teacher said. His words jolted me back to the present where I was still crying and quite curious as to why Delilah was silent next to me all that time. When I looked over at her, she was rocking back and forth with her mouth moving really fast, and she kept talking about "coming in a Honda".

When I looked around, I noticed everyone was doing the same thing. They were talking really fast or mumbling out loud. Some of them were also coming in Hondas, while others were buying Toyotas. I used to hear my mother speaking that same stuff when she had her parties in the basement, but I attributed it to her being drunk or something. But I was in a bible study, so no one should have been drunk as far as I knew. Even though it all sounded like confusion to me, it made perfect sense to my feet as they once again moved on their own and landed me right in front of the bible study leader. Even though there were other people at the altar, the leader kept looking at me. I wasn't quite sure what I wanted while I was up there. Did I need to be prayed for? Did I need more olive oil put on my forehead? The leader prayed for each person one by one, skipping over me and continuing with the others. There was a person standing behind me who squeezed both of my arms as if to say, "Don't move."

After a while, the people at the altar returned to their seats. Some even began filing out of the building. I was still at the altar waiting for something to happen or for someone to tell me if something *should* happen. All I remembered was that I was standing there crying, confused, wondering how did I get up there in the first place, was Delilah still in her seat speaking gibberish about automobiles, and if the jesus cloud was outside waiting for me.

"Everyone stretch your hands this way."

"This way" meant towards me and I found myself in the middle of a circle with everyone stretching their hands in my direction like Hitler was in the room. Then all of a sudden, I felt something like a bolt of lightning hit me and I was on the floor. I kept hearing this buzzing sound in my ears like a dull whir that sounded like gears were turning. I had never experienced anything like it before, but for some reason I was not afraid.

After the bolt and the noise, I began to move uncontrollably as though I was having seizures. The voices of the people surrounding me were growing louder and louder, and I kept hearing, "Come out of her! Come out of her!" And the more they said it, the more I began to notice a sound in the background like knives were sharpening. I knew what it was.

"In Jesus' name!" a male voice yelled. At the sound of that name, my body lurched forward and I threw up something horrible. It tasted like the smell of sulfur, and when I looked on the ground, there was something black and scaly in the middle of the goo. I didn't remember eating anything black or scaly that day. I kept throwing up from the front and from the back. I was feeling violently ill and wondered if anyone was going to call an ambulance. I could not lift my body up off the floor, and I remember trying to get out of the circle by crawling my way around. I was on my belly with my arms at my sides, and although I was able to move forward, I still couldn't raise myself up from the floor.

I was still in the midst of what I thought was confusion and I felt like my body was being pulled apart like there was a fight for parts of me. I recognized the voice of The Blacksmith and he seemed to be protesting. I remember hearing him say he was there by permission and had been there for years. He was on assignment and was not yet finished. He had some cutting to do and did not intend to leave until he was down to the last slice.

"Come out of her!"

"No!"

"Satan, you are a liar! Come out of her!"

"I belong here! I have permission!"

"By the authority of Jesus Christ, you will obey!"

"I have permission!"

"Sister, repeat these words after me."

It was the bible study teacher leading the charge against The Blacksmith, and he placed his hands on my belly and kept telling me what to say. It took all of my strength to repeat the lines stating that I renounce all witchcraft and familiar spirits, that I reject the spirit of violence, anger, and bitterness, and that I cast down every evil imagination in the name of jesus christ. And once again, at the sound of the name of jesus, I lurched forward and threw up again. At that moment I jumped to my feet and began screaming, asking jesus to save me.

"That's it! That's it! Call on him!" someone in the circle urged.

"jesus! Help me! Help me!"

Every time I said "jesus", my tongue burned and the sharpening knives grew louder and louder. I kept calling on him and the knives kept sharpening, and they did not stop until I said, "Jesus, I believe in you. You are God!"

And with that, I let out a loud scream that seemed to come from my toes as I fell to my knees. A door slammed shut in my mind, then I heard a nail being banged into the door. The Blacksmith had nailed a note to me written in angry, bleeding, crimson letters. It read "I SHALL RETURN".

It seemed as though I was in the Student Center forever, but I did not mind. I liked the clean feeling I felt inside, even though on the outside I was not so fresh because of the liquids in my body being purged all at once. Delilah led me to the bathroom where I was able to clean up. There was no change of clothes for me, so I wound up wearing a white sheet that covered a table with a gold plate on it, and one of the brothers gave me a button-up shirt he wore over his tee. Everyone was looking at me with that, "Is she alright?" look.

"What happened to me?" I asked, directing my questions to no one and everyone at the same time. The bible study leader was the first to speak. He began by first asking me what faith I previously belonged to, about my family and home life, where did we come from, etc. They all seemed irrelevant questions which I chose to vaguely answer until he began to explain what took place while I was at the altar.

"In essence you were in bondage to a witchcraft spirit."

He continued by saying how that particular spirit acts like a python by squeezing the life out of you and whispering deceptive things in your ears. He asked about my family history to see if there was anyone in my home who delved in witchcraft. I had to admit that my mother did some dark deeds that she thought worked and my grandmother was considered a Sopper, but I never gave credence to the stories.

"Well, your mother's dealings had a hold on you and that's why you always had trouble in your mind with bad daydreams. It's also why when you were on the floor, you slithered around like a snake and couldn't lift yourself up until that hold was broken off of you."

My first mind told me not to believe a word he was saying, but I could not deny what I experienced. And I think it had to happen in such a dramatic way because I was so sure all of that stuff my mother did was hocus pocus. But I could not wrap my mind around believing my mother was the source of the things I could not articulate.

"And I don't know what it is exactly," he continued, "but you had a very strong spirit guarding you. I think your mother sent a watchman to be with you wherever you went to make sure that once you left her presence, you would not seek God."

"How can she do that?" I asked.

"There are many ways it can be done."

He continued by explaining people who deal in witchcraft usually have a spirit guide who is at their beck and call, and those guides stay in the family. Eventually that same guide would fall on me to do what my family had been doing in the basement for years. He said depending on what culture a person is from, that spirit takes on many names. He said he felt it was a demon god of iron and warfare, opponent of Michael, one of God's angels.

"Towards the end, I heard a door slam shut in the spirit, which is the realm we can't see unless it is revealed to us by God. That spirit that left you is angry," the leader said.

"And he will return," I mumbled to myself, remembering the note I saw in my mind. The demon god revealed: The Blacksmith.

"If you were sincere about confessing Christ you have protection. That spirit can and will return in order to test you, but he cannot harm you. You are under the divine protection of the Holy Ghost. When you receive Jesus Christ as your Lord and Savior, the Holy Spirit will fill your heart and mind and teach you The Way. Are you truly ready to give Christ your whole life, thoughts, actions, speech, and all?"

I was ready because I was desperate for some kind of relief. I could not deny that something happened to me and that the only time something happened to me was in the presence of people like Delilah. As much as I hated to admit it, maybe the Christians had it right after all.

And with that I recited what was called The Sinner's Prayer, received Christ in my heart, and then something else happened. My lips began to move uncontrollably like Delilah's and the other people's mouths earlier that evening. What came out of me sounded like a beautiful language, none like I had ever heard before. Every few phrases some English would break through until I finally threw up my hands and shouted in a deep, guttural voice, "THIS-HOUSE-IS-CLEAN! THIS-HOUSE-IS-CLEAN!" No one had to tell me what was happening.

"Welcome to the family of God!" Delilah exclaimed with tears in her eyes. "Thank you Jesus!"

Everyone began hugging me, and even though I was newly converted and feeling good, I wasn't quite ready to be all loving and what not. One day at a time was good enough for me. As we gathered our belongings to leave, the Bible study leader looked at me with a strange look.

"Did you say your family name?" he asked.

"Paternal Meyers, maternal Toval."

"Hmm, okay thanks," he replied. "I'm Michael Tibideau, campus pastor of The Way Ministries. Welcome."

I didn't like the sound of "Hmm, okay thanks", but I was in no mood to read into anything. I had to let the suspicions go in order to clear my mind to really understand all that happened to me. It seemed like overnight I went from believing in nothing, with exposure to hocus pocus, to believing in something knowing the hocus pocus was real. That was something I could not wrap my brain around. All of it was happening too fast and there was no Mari around to help me figure it out. Maybe if I called her and let her know I was a Christian now, she'd be my friend again.

Delilah briefed me on what my next steps as a new Christian would be. That was the part that made me nervous. I had forgotten that with this Christian stuff, there might be a part two that would have me looking glazed over like Delilah and telling people how to live or that might make people hate me for reasons that have nothing to do with me personally and everything to do with me spiritually. In short, as a Christian I would reap what I've sown in other Christians before that night. The thought made me wince at the backlash.

My first step as a new Christian, ironically, was not to join a church. I was supposed to go, but there was no pressure for membership until I understood what the Bible asked of me and if I was publicly own it by getting baptized. I had to begin cultivating a relationship with God by praying, fasting, reading, and not being ashamed of sharing my faith.

"And all of this is supposed to happen how soon?" I asked, battling my cynicism that seemed to slowly reappear with each foot that distanced us from the altar. Delilah did not miss a beat.

"It's not about how fast or slow things will happen. Everybody is different. I want you to remember this if you remember nothing else, that this life is a process. It is not some overnight thing where your problems magically disappear. This is an honest life's work for heavenly wages."

Delilah's words kept playing in my head over and over like a scratched record. That was the part that scared me. I was at the point of change, but I didn't want to change so fast that I wouldn't recognize myself and not so slow that whatever was in me before would come back with a vengeance. I thought the religion thing was supposed to come easy, but it was evident that there was no magic spell to help expedite things. The experience would have to be lived one day at a time.

The part that troubled me most was what my mother would think. Every time I ever heard her talk about Christians it was never in a good light. For one, she only saw them as people to steal gifts from because that was her only exposure growing up. When she became old enough to do what my grandmother did, she got with her friend Rita in order to learn rituals rather than operate as her own entity as my grandmother did. My grandmother seemed proud to let everyone know she was a Sopper. My mother, on the other hand, wasn't strictly trying to help anyone figure out their future at first. She claimed all the stuff she did was for protection against people who would try to harm her or retaliate against her for whatever offense they claimed was done to them. My mother was particularly vigilant against people in the churches where my grandmother would hop to sop because they knew what she was up to and would pray against her. She would drill into me, "Suzi baby, those women in Pentecost Sunday white! Ugh! You got to steer clear of them. I mean steer clear!"

My mother would tell me stories of the women in white whom she called, "Holy Sanctified Women", who did nothing but pray and not eat in order to keep the pastor safe from witches. She said they would speak, what I learned after Bible study, to be tongues. Sometimes they would see into the future like she claimed my grandmother did. They would walk around my grandmother's yard singing and throwing salt on the ground, quoting the Bible and saying something about Jesus and blood. My mother said every time those women came, my grandmother would get sick, and when she came out of it, she seemed to have more gray hair than she did before they came.

"The Lord has spoken. He is going to stop your line!" one of the ladies pronounced during a prayer vigil against my grandmother. "God is going to raise up a seed and that seed is going to put an end to your curses. In Jesus' name!"

When the Holy Sanctified Woman said that, my grandmother fell back, looked into my mother's face, and said, "I curse your womb. Child or no child, you will never be a mother!" to which the church lady replied, "The Lord has spoken. The Holy Spirit has cast His shadow. The child will be born. And if the child is motherless still, the Bible says when your mother and father forsake you, the Lord will take you up! Higher Higher Higher in Jesus! Yes suh! Let man be liar and let God be true!"

Even though I was still not ready to accept all of the stories as true, I could see how my mother fulfilled the prediction in a way. She never would settle down with my father, who was the only man who really loved her. In her younger days she went from man to man—although to her credit they never got any free milk—which never allowed us to have a nuclear home life. After the last man she brought home, Rose Gold, tried to violate our home, she stopped dating altogether and only allowed men into the house who were part of her black magic group. And even then, she would only let them in only when Federline was around.

"God, help me understand what happened to me. Help me get through this. I don't know what to ask for. I just know I can't do this by myself. Please help me, and please bring my friend Mari back. She's the only one who understands me. And, I know this is bad, but I'm not ready for all of those church people to be touching on me and smiling in my face. I need more time. Amen."

No sooner than had I said "Amen", the phone rang. It was already way past midnight. I almost tackled the phone like a linebacker hoping it was Mari.

"I see you ain't been steering clear."

"Ma? Hey."

"I said I see you ain't been steering clear," my mother repeated.

"Of what?"

"Thanks to you I'm having a sleepless night and got two more strands of gray. I was woken out my sleep by something dressed in white wrestling me to the ground, calling your name out, and talking about some clean house. Now my womb hurts."

"What are you talking about?"

"If *you* don't know, *I* don't know."

Before I could get another word out, my mother hung up the phone. My mind raced to find out what was going on in my life that precipitated all of that divine intervention in such a short span of time. One minute I had no attachment to any faith other than head knowledge and a few teenaged trips to Mari's church. Then I went to college and after three years, found myself inducted into some sort of society that knew more about me than I did, and in some way my mother was connected. How did she know what happened to me? How could all of those events be real?

I tried to recall moments from my childhood that might give a clue as to when all of the sorcery type events took place and what happened in the house that seemed stranger than normal. But for my house, strange *was* normal. I remembered a time when I was about five and my mother took me to my Aunt Camille's house because she had to go to some party, much like the ones she would have in the basement of our house. Camille was the eldest by ten years and didn't come around too much. She and my mother, who was the middle child, didn't get along. My mother used to be afraid of Camille because during their teenaged years, she was more ruthless than she and Reesie combined. My mother told me stories of how Camille would lock her and Reesie in the basement with skeletons of real people then whoop on them if she heard them scream. Camille worked in the medical field and often paid people to give her body parts they should have disposed of, or got one of the homeless people who slept in the graveyard to steal a body.

One night my mother said she thought she lost her mind because she was afraid to scream, but she was also afraid of being in the basement with the remains. In order to alleviate the fear, she and Reesie made a pact that they would "call out to the night", and whatever evil was in the darkness would befriend them and they'd never be afraid again. That was when a woman appeared before her, who she later acknowledged was Madame Samedi, and she said she would teach my mother how to use her untapped powers while she would let Reesie decide what she wanted from the dark. Reesie said she wanted to be like a movie star from one of the black and white movies she watched on T.V., not realizing the actress she was asking to be like was less than stellar in real life. That was when Reesie went from hard to get to easy to throw away.

When the pair agreed to open up to whatever the darkness would offer them, my mother said one of the skeletons sat up and turned to them saying, "Would you please tell my family the devil is real?" My mother said ever since then, she never feared anyone or anything, while Reesie became morally reckless abusing alcohol, cocaine, and men, just like the movie star she idolized.

After that night, the tables turned and Camille became my mother's victim. Camille was in a car accident and her right femur was shattered. When my mother visited Camille in the hospital, she carried with her a black bag. She gave Camille a knowing look and said, "In case the doctors can't fix your leg back, tell them to try this one." Camille knew what it was and summoned security to remove my mother, and the femur and tibia she carried in her bag, out of her room. Before my mother exited the room, Camille screamed, "Well done, you she-devil! Bone for bone!"

I recalled another memory of my other aunt, Reesie, on the phone talking in front of me, not realizing that age five was old enough to store events in the mind and make meaning out of them. She said my mother was taking up my grandmother's ways for evil and that it was going to bring about a horrible death if she didn't stop. She talked about the men that came in and out of the house and how most of them were under some kind of spell. I remember how strange it was that every time my mother invited a man over for dinner, she would always cook something with red sauce. I asked her why and she would say that red was the color of seduction, but according to my aunt, my mother would put some of her feminine fluids in the sauce, speak a spell over it, and that would make the man give her anything she wanted.

"Esther gonna kill herself, you see...Yes, I know what I'm saying, hear me good... Uh huh, you right. She trying to be momma but she ain't nowhere near that. Nowhere," my aunt said to the unknown person on the other end of the phone. "She got the power but she ain't doing right with it. It's my fault and I can't make it right...See, I done said something about it and she got mad and made a doll on me...Shucks no, I ain't never scared. I got some magic too. That's why after all of that saucing and greasing she can't keep a man 'cause I bought some man shoes, and every time she bring that child of hers over here I know what's up...that's right. Show time! I take out them man shoes and spit in them real good. I curse them fools good! She might get the money and the pearls first, but after while I get something too...the last laugh..Say what now?...No, she don't know it's me...Yea, I went straight to the point of origin and got the Magic Man to make me a cloak...Yea, a cloak...You dummy, you in this too and don't know what a cloak is?...It's when you get the Magic Man to ask the spirits to hide you so nobody knows what you doing to them and they can't ever find out...How I do that? Now if I tell you, what's the point of my cloak? You a dumb somebody!...What you say?...Yea, she over here today...No, she don't know nothing...Yea, Esther got her blood taken at the point of origin. That child under a curse just so somebody can make a doll and stick a pin in it...Yup...Tit for tat with them spirits. You make a doll, they wanna take a doll. A *living* doll...Alright, let me quit this business and send you off my ears. You done ruined my day talking all this hookamuh tutu."

My aunt hung up the phone and blazed one to calm her nerves. Even though she pretended to not be afraid of my mother, she really was. She realized I was across the room staring at her and asked me what did I hear her say.

"Nothing," I answered.

"Good. You don't never hear nothing, hear me?"

I didn't answer.

"You learnin'."

I fell asleep hoping everything that happened at the Bible study Friday night had been one big dream. I didn't even care if it was a premature daymare that was early for its torturous appointment. I just needed to feel as though I had a grip on my life. I was new in the Christian thing and already I was looking for normalcy, even if it was a dysfunctional one.

I was a bundle of nervous energy due to my confusion, and the only way I knew to drain my energy was to lash out. But I knew that was not a good way to handle things anymore since I denounced anger and bitterness in front of the whole world during Bible study. The closest I could come to letting off steam was to try to call Charisse again to see if maybe she had calmed down. Talking about her situation would allow me to say, "I told you so" in a nice way. That would help calm the urge in me to go off. It was a shame that the only reason I wanted to call was to see the damage done from Charisse not heeding my warnings. I guess that would be deceptive. A person thinks the call is out of genuine concern when the reality is the caller just wants to see how bad off the person is and confirm the results of that person's stupidity for not listening.

As I reached for the phone, I knocked over my Bible. When I picked it up, it was open to a verse in Proverbs 14:17 that the person who used it before me had highlighted. It talked about people who are easily angered do foolish things. Instead of calling Charisse, I called Delilah. She conveniently made sure I had every means to contact her before we parted ways last night.

"That's just God's way of talking to you. What verse was it?" Delilah inquired.

"I just wanted to ask."

"Sometimes God talks to you through the Bible, other times through people, dreams, and a whole lot of other ways. Sometimes when a person is a new Christian the Lord will be very overt in order to seal you in. But as you grow, you have to learn how to listen for his voice in ways that aren't so obvious. You do that by spending a lot of time in prayer to know what it feels like to be in his presence, and by reading the Bible so that you know what kinds of things he'd say."

I had more questions for Delilah such as how did she become a Christian and how did she know so much, but I wanted to relax a little more and take inventory of my own life to see how my decision would impact me for the long haul. I decided to take a long walk to clear my mind.

There was a nature path near campus where a lot of people walked to get to the lake. I always loved walking past the flowers and daydreaming about each one turning into a friend of mine. They would talk to me in hushed, flowery tones about their perfect lives, their breath smelling like sweet perfume and the air from their speech tickling every part of me that giggled. They would whisper about how much the sun loved them, how the sky loved them so much so that it left dew for them to drink in the morning, and that the grass protected them like towering sentinels so that when they slept, they had someplace to nestle in safety.

There was a particular patch I liked to visit where the flowers were all totally different hues. I would use my floral telepathy to tell them if I was mad or sad, and that I was desperate for someone to treat me special, to love and protect me, leave dew for me to drink in the morning, and give me someplace to nestle in peace. They would just look at me in a very apathetic manner as if to say, "That's too bad!" then go back to their business of being admired. They were too radiant and beautiful to bother with me. They had more important things to do than to be weighed down by me and my imperfections. It was clear I would never win them over, but I still wanted to try. By the time I finished thinking about my clinginess to apathetic flowers, I arrived at my favorite patch. I hadn't been there in a while and they looked nowhere near the way I remember. They were all the same color and looked as though they were dying from neglect. There were even facing another direction that let me know they had turned their backs on me.

I decided to keep walking to find something new to fixate on for I was clearly violating every person, space, and flower I came in contact with. But the flowers had a right to turn from me. My love affair with them, my deep admiration and want for their attention, was a metaphor for the sister I never had, the one person I could always find to answer my questions, to provide the stability she made me realize I didn't have. Mari epitomized everything I needed to aspire to—or at least thought I did. I didn't want to aspire to her need to lie to me and make me believe our friendship was built on sand.

"People change. Always have, always will," my mother would say. I was reminded of her belief that at some point Mari, Charisse, and I would part ways once we got to college.

"Every ten, fifteen years—I need to play those numbers—people go through a cycle where they change their, what you call it?"

"Mentality," I answered flatly while eating a bowl of lentil soup.

"Yes. Mentality. It's like…see this puff of smoke here?" my mother pointed as she blew rings of smoke in my direction. "You see how they float toward you and when they get closer, they disappear?"

"Yeah."

"It's not that the smoke is actually disappearing. It's still there, but as it travels along, see, it changes form and now you can't recognize if it is what it was when they started out. That's how people are, so get used to it."

I began to cough as the disappearing people made their way into my nostrils.

"Uh huh! They do that too. Change up to the point they make you choke on 'em. Kill your spirit, even. That's people."

I realized it wasn't a cigarette she was smoking and my recognition made her laugh.

"I see your nose is working!" my mother said as she noted my swift recovery from a bad cold. "Hurry up and eat before you catch a contact. Ain't no free high's in this house!"

Again she laughed, but harder than the first round of laughter and at my expense. She was in her usual spot wearing her pink robe and open-toed slippers, rollers in her hair, a smoke in one hand, legs parted at a 45 degree angle, and the Dream Book pamphlet spread out in front of her. She always looked at that pamphlet to get her numbers. I remember every month it was published it would be a different color, and at the top right corner there would be a caricature of a black man with a short afro saying, "Big Snook's Number of the Day is…"

"Hot dog!" my mother exclaimed when she felt she landed on a number that would make her hit. "Thank you! I got to burn a candle! Give me my lighter and the phone, Sue Baby. We about to hit!"

The way she emphasized "hit" was like the sound of a suction toy or piece of clay being thrown onto a white wall, and hoping it'd stick for a while before peeling itself off and plopping on the floor. And with my mother's weird luck, nothing ever fell off the wall.

Despite the spiritual high I was on the night before, I had sense enough to know what goes up must come down. I still had to think about graduation and if there would be more business with campus police. If I did graduate, what would happen next? I didn't apply to any graduate schools. Matter of fact, I didn't even think about it. I figured I'd go home, get a job, and go with the flow. But if I go home a Christian, what would happen between my mother and me? Would she try to sop me? Would she put that spirit on me again? Was all of it real?

By the time I finished my train of thought, I was back on campus and standing behind a familiar person in line at the dining hall; it was Mari. I wasn't sure if I should speak or not, but I was eager to tell her I went to Bible study and became a Christian. Maybe she'd feel guilty for lying to me about our friendship and confess it really was her mother who convinced her to end it. I decided to tap her on the shoulder. She turned around and acted shocked to see me, like she was hiding and was found out.

"Hey Mari," I said in the lightest way possible. "What's on the menu?"

It was obvious I was nervous and trying to make small talk. She didn't buy any of it, but I continued talking anyway. "You know I went to Bible study and became a Christian. I think I won't be angry anymore."

Mari just looked at me and smiled, giving me one of those, "Oh, that's really nice but who cares?" looks. My nervousness wouldn't let me quit.

"They told me a whole bunch of stuff about my mother and me and my anger issues. I think my life is going to be different from now on. I won't be a burden to you. You know, giving me advice all the time and stuff. You won't have to worry about that."

Mari finally decided to answer. In hindsight I wished she hadn't.

"That's good. It's about time."

I couldn't stand the coolness. As much as I was trying to be transparent after she laid me out, as much as I was making a fool out of myself to get her to see I was okay, it was as though she couldn't care less.

"Mari, what did I do so wrong to you? What did I do?"

"Suzi, you just don't get it. Leave it alone! I said what I had to say before, alright? Leave it alone."

There I was standing in the line holding on to a tray with both my hands, standing stock still like a guard at Buckingham Palace with tears flooding to my eyes. I felt so embarrassed about selling my soul to someone who no longer wanted to be bothered with me. I was so desperate for her friendship that I put my business on full blast while hanging in a chow line and kept talking even though Mari clearly didn't care. I was slowly but surely losing my spiritual high from the night before. I thought the buzz would last a little bit longer, but apparently not. And what else was apparent was that for the first time I had been on that campus, I would be eating alone.

After I got my food, I surveyed the room to see if anyone I had ignored all those years, in my loyalty to the two people who no longer called me their friend, would give me a welcoming look. I began to feel like everyone in the room was my enemy. I looked to my left and saw Naziir, who I felt should not have let anything happen in his room he wouldn't do. I looked to my right and saw Rooms 509 and 513 chatting away. I looked left again and saw the alpha beta gamma delta girl who rejected me a long time ago. I killed her so many times in my mind that I was almost surprised to see her breathing. I guess not all dreams come true. Then I even saw The Gabber. I guess I didn't hit him in the throat hard enough because he was wolfing down the same thing I had on my plate. Instead of making a fool out of myself and looking like a lonely reject, I decided to get some carryout boxes to bring my food back to the room. That was until Chuck stopped me.

"Come sit with us, Sister."

Somewhat embarrassed that I was about to sit with the very people I tried to avoid less than 48 hours ago, I tried to bridle my feelings and just let things play themselves out. I sat down with Chuck and a few other people I recognized from the Bible study. They all were staring and smiling at me with that "bless her heart" look.

As we ate, Chuck was rattling away about how blessed he was to see me at the study—that for me to come out on a Friday night meant I was really looking for God. Not one to like to talk while I ate, I couldn't if I wanted to. While Chuck talked, I noticed his eyes and his lips. His eyes seemed to dance as he spoke, and his lips were moving slowly and deliberately, like he chose his words as carefully as he chose his fruit. Every few sentences I asked him a question He was from Germantown, Tennessee. His family was originally from Chattanooga, and they had a church there until he said God told his father to install someone to take his place and do missions trips to impoverished countries. When his family returned to the US, they moved to southwest Tennessee to be near Memphis, better known to his family as Pentecostal headquarters. His father felt being there would help him learn a type of Christianity that included powerful works, not just sermonizing and shaking people's hands. He was seeking the ministry Jesus had and felt that particular group would season him more than his own denomination.

"It really caused a divide in my family. They said he was crazy for even associating with them because our denomination was conservative. We had a few people who were charismatics…"

"What?" I asked.

"Charismatics. People who believe in the supernatural gifts of God and their operation for modern times. You saw it last night."

"I don't know anything about that stuff."

I was still processing. Chuck was going too fast for me by telling me more than I wanted to be responsible for. Chuck finally realized his conversation was startling me and changed the subject, but not before he mentioned his parents were considered outcasts for taking their faith to another level, which led him to go away to school to get away from it all. As far as his relatives were concerned—even his Christian relatives—he and his parents were dead.

When he said "dead", the word leapt into my mouth and got stuck in my throat. No amount of water, throat clearing, or mother's luck could get it to slide off the wall. I looked at the others at the table and no one seemed to flinch at talk of outcasts and death. By the time I finished my food, I felt I had died a hundred deaths. Everyone and everything was killing me that day.

I quickly scooped up my tray and wanted to exit without saying goodbye. I had to get away from those people before whatever they had jumped on me. I felt like I had been inducted into something I wouldn't be able to get out of and that would never leave me because I knew too much too soon. It wasn't even a full 24 hours and already I was looking for a get out of jail free card. I was a prisoner of what some people called the truth. My mind would not stop racing with questions that scared me more than the answers. *How do I change my mind about this thing after all that scary stuff that happened to me? How do I go to God and say I said all those words that night because I was desperate? Would I have become a Christian if my life were perfect?* My thoughts were more desperate than ever.

"You'll be alright!" Chuck said as he tried to touch my arm, but I was too quick for him as I scooted out of my seat and hurried out the door. I didn't walk fast enough, apparently, because he caught up with me and asked where I was going. Chuck just wanted to remind me that church was tomorrow, but they weren't going to meet on campus. The pastor was going to be a guest at a larger church out in the country somewhere. He told me he would have Delilah come to my room and show me where everyone was catching the charter bus.

While Chuck talked, he noticed I was shaking. He put his hand on my shoulder and began to pray out loud and in public. My thoughts told me I really got into something crazy.

"Father," he prayed. "I lift up my sister, Suzi. Lord God, you know how she feels and how new all of this is to her. I ask you, Father, to help her learn your ways and to accept people's care and attention. Lord God help her understand that she does not have to earn it but that it comes free. Take away the spirit of fear that will hinder her from coming into all knowledge. Open her heart so that she will receive all the goodness that comes with accepting your Son. In Jesus' name. Amen."

*Who is Lord God? Father? And then he said something about Jesus? All of those people mentioned for one prayer?*

"Suzi, it's going to be alright. You will learn and understand."

"Will you people stop reading my mind! Is *new Christian* synonymous with *no privacy*?!"

I ran away from Chuck as fast as I could. I was part angry that he was in my head—like what everyone else seemed to be doing the night before—and part embarrassed that people who knew me to be a non-believer in religious things and a budding hellion saw me praying with a Holy Roller. My soul was saved, but I apparently couldn't save my face.

As promised, the next morning Delilah was at the door knocking like the building was on fire. She had been standing there for ten minutes while I was under the covers trying not to breathe. There was an interval where she would stop and I'd see the shadow of her feet move away, but then she'd come back. When the shadow returned, I heard a key in the door.

"WAIT!" I screamed. She had gotten the housemaster to check on me because she thought something had happened. I lit her up like a firecracker. "How are you coming in here like that?"

"Well, you were expecting me and you didn't answer. I heard movement and thought you might not have been able to answer the door," Delilah explained.

"First of all, I didn't tell nobody nothing! I ain't say I was going nowhere with nobody at no time!" I said in my best vernacular. I was beginning to sound like my mother. The housemaster looked embarrassed and Delilah didn't move a muscle. She acted like I yelled sour somethings in her ears.

"I'll wait while you get ready."

"I can't believe this malarkey!"

I was fuming while Delilah sat in my room oblivious to the fact that despite being invited the previous night, her invitation was revoked. I didn't even know what I wanted to wear. I deliberately took my time looking and holding up each piece, saying, "No, this isn't good enough", then throwing them on the bed. By the time I was done, I had every drawer emptied and the closet was about to follow suit. Delilah wasn't buying the act.

"You can wear jeans. You can wear sweats. You can wear your nightgown. You can wear whatever. Come as you are and Jesus will come as he is."

"Persistent little booger," I snarled under my breath. I left the room to take a shower then returned fully dressed.

"I'm ready. Let's go to the shindig."

"We have an hour before we have to leave for the bus."

My face clearly read, "Then what are you doing here right now?" and when I looked at Delilah, I realized she was a smarter cookie than I previously thought. She knew I'd be resistant to going to church and came extra early to make sure she'd be able to navigate my hiccups. I had to give her respect for being shrewd. I wanted to know more about her as my curiosity still not satisfied from our first real encounter when I discovered the divinity of clouds. I tried to calm myself down, realizing no matter what I said or how I acted, Delilah would not flinch. I tried to make small talk, which was my way of saying I was sorry for giving her a hard time. At that moment a thought came to me.

"Hey! Since we have time, let's go to Charisse's room and see if she wants to go with us." Delilah's eyes lit up at the thought of possibly converting another person. She readily agreed.

I was shocked at myself for even allowing that thought to enter into my mind. Charisse would probably be resistant because we were on the outs and since then she had no idea I got religion. Even though her family went to church from time to time, it really wasn't her thing. She hated that her father was always rubbing elbows with the deacons and staying after church waiting for someone to point out to him which middle-aged woman was desperate, uncoupled, and looking for a man to rescue her from the single life. Charisse equated church to a pickup spot. I remember she told me about a woman in the choir, Sister Flora, who had eyes on her father. In order to get his attention, she began to sing over the person who had the lead. While the lead soloist sang, she kept looking behind her to hear who was belting out tunes louder than she was. It was Sister Flora. Everyone in the congregation just kept going with it, thinking maybe it was "The Spirit moving her." The Spirit eventually moved her to step all the way up to the front and grab an unattended microphone. Sister Flora went into the congregation and began singing directly to Charisse's father saying, "Don't let your blessings pass you by cause when it's gone it's gone. Don't let your blessings pass you by, make sure you hear from the Lord. He wants to bless you, to open your eyes and restore you. He wants to bless you, and it is right here standing before you."

Everyone clearly knew she was ad libbing, but they were so busy being enthralled by what they thought was God that they didn't notice she had motives. By the time she finished singing, the whole church was up in a frenzy saying how God moved and they never heard her sing like that. *Weird*. Stories like that, coupled with my mother's accounts of The Adventures of Granny the Sopper, didn't endear me to church at all, yet I was about to set foot in one located way out in the country that may have more circus acts than I've ever seen or heard about.

By the time I realized I was about to step into another argument, we were already at Charisse's dorm room knocking on the door. Surprisingly she answered, fixing her robe to cover herself since she had no belt. I let Delilah speak because it seemed like she had good practice talking to people even when they didn't want to speak to her. She apologized for coming unannounced, and explained how we were on our way to church and thought it would be a good idea to bring a friend who might enjoy the service. She said we had time to wait for her to get ready if she was willing to go.

As Delilah continued to speak, I noticed Charisse's eyes were red and swollen, and there were beer cans strewn all around the room. I even saw an open Bible on her desk and a little note sticking out of one of the pages with what looked like dried brown stains on it.

"Yea, I'll go."

While I stood there in shock, Delilah looked as though she fully expected Charisse to acquiesce. Either it was another one of those Christian mind reading tricks or I was just plain out of the loop. Either way, I was happy to have a chance to catch up with Charisse since we had not spoken since our blowup over the phone.

I was hoping Charisse would leave us in the room while she took a shower in the common bathroom, but she took a washcloth and wet it with bottled water, then hit the hot spots right in front of us. That was one of the things I didn't like about Charisse; she was immodest. She'd do or say anything, anytime, anywhere, and for the life of her could never understand why people didn't respect her. Sometimes I wondered why I even did. I remember the first time Charisse spent a few nights with me while we were in junior high and my mother noticed she never took a shower. When my mother told her to wash up, Charisse took several sheets of paper towel, wet them in the kitchen sink, and wiped her face, underarms, and feet.

"Ain't you gonna get *the cat*? I can hear that thing howling on the fence from way down the street!"

Instead of excusing herself, Charisse began to lift up her skirt at which my mother hollered, "Get your aromatic self up to the bathroom!" then turned to me and said, "Nasty wench, that's what she is, heard me? Somebody been touching on that child. I bet you it's that no good black daddy of hers with his two tufts of hair. Bald as an eagle trying to salvage two tufts. Imagine that!"

One thing my mother did not have was couth. Another thing she did not have was an indoor voice. I asked her to show some respect for my friend since she was at our house for refuge. My mother didn't care as she continued to rant that Charisse smelled like sex and that she can tell it was sex with a relative because incest has its own scent.

After Charisse went back home, my mother burned incense in fragrances like jasmine and sandalwood in every room, then went down to the basement for a long time. When she came back up the stairs, she handed me a bag and asked me to bury it in the ground and then put a trash can on top of it. After I got outside, I looked in the bag and saw it was a doll in the likeness of Bozo the Clown, except the red hair he usually had on the sides were burned off and the smile he usually had was blacked out on the corners and replaced with a frown. My mother said the doll was Charisse's father. She said just like he stole Charisse's glory, she was going to steal his two tufts of glory. When I asked her why I had to bury the doll and put the trash can on top of it, she said it was because he was less than garbage and she always wanted him to be reminded of the stench he put on his daughter.

What the doll was supposed to do I didn't know, but my mother seemed to think she exacted revenge and felt it was confirmed when Charisse's father tried to put in a mild relaxer to make his sides look like he had Cherokee in the family. After leaving it on too long, he burned his scalp to the point where the Cherokee Maker left scabs. Since then his tufts only grew back in patches and he eventually accepted he was bald for good.

There was never any proof Charisse was molested other than the hint she gave me our last night at home before leaving for college, but if she was, it would explain why she had an obsession with male attention and an aversion to soap and water at times. It would also explain why no matter how many times she ran to our house because of something her father did, she would always turn sympathetic and go back home like nothing happened. "That's how fighting lovers act," my mother would say. "Nasty! All of fifty 'em. I wonder if his kids double as his grandkids."

At the thought I let out a chuckle that caused Delilah to give me a funny look and Charisse to give me a knowing look. I saw something different in her eyes, though, something that said, "I hate you but help me because you're the only one who ever would." I moved my gaze a little lower to her wrist where I noticed a large leather cuff she was careful to not disturb while she was hitting the hot spots. It was then I realized the kind of help she needed. It was the kind of help that would keep her from getting brown spots on pieces of paper. I guess she figured after she heard about Vince, she may as well hasten her death.

That day was not the first time I saw brown spots. Charisse had been suicidal since she was in elementary school. The first time she came to my house after an attempt was when her mother died, which was one of the most hilarious moments in my life. She saw in a movie that this lady took a bunch of pills and went to sleep forever. Charisse grabbed the biggest white bottle she saw with the biggest pills and thought ten or so would do the trick. She walked to my house hoping she would fall out in the street on the way, thus being true to her need for attention and drama. By the time she reached my house, she thought she was closer to death and decided to start confessing her heart, thinking she would not live long enough to deal with the repercussions.

"First of all, Suzi, let me tell you," Charisse said with her speech slurring seemingly on purpose and not due to any real speech impairment. "I love you and everything, but you need to stop acting like you my mother. And yea me, you, and Mari are friends, but the truth is I don't like her. I never liked her. When I die..."

"When you what?" I asked in disbelief.

"When I die you gonna miss me because I am the only real friend you got. Everybody your friend because they scared of your momma."

"Somebody talkin' 'bout me up in here?" my mother inquired in a tone that let us know she was ready to set somebody straight.

"Miss Esther, I love you like a mother," Charisse confessed while fake slurring. "But..."

But before Charisse had a chance to finish, she had a sudden urge to go to the bathroom and shouted, "I took a bottle of pills and I'm about to die!" After a few seconds of hearing Niagara Falls in my toilet, Charisse let out a loud scream and hollered, "It's glowing green! It's glowing green!"

My mother went to the bathroom to investigate and I followed suit. She looked in the toilet, sniffed real hard, and laughed harder than I ever heard her laugh.

"Sue, your friend is all kinds of stupid. So dumb she can't even die right. How the hell you gonna die from too much Vitamin C?"

Apparently Charisse overdosed on vitamins while thinking it was a bottle of sleeping pills. And after my mother stopped laughing, her face straightened and she turned to Charisse.

"Now back to what you was saying before you neon-greened my bathroom. You love me like a mother but what?"

I didn't stick around to see the aftermath. I heard the bathroom door close and the sound of a wild animal nearly breaking the door off the hinges trying to get out. I also heard my mother stuttering between licks, "Don't-you-ever-come-in-my-house-talkin'-'bout..."

An eerie feeling came over me that made me wish Charisse had succeed in killing herself back then. I didn't know if it was my own maliciousness because of our discord or because I heard another *bang*. What I did know that Charisse didn't was that I envied her courage. I wish I had the guts to take my own life too, but something told me there was something about the next day that always made a person want to try again. However, I knew at some point one of us might succeed and I didn't know which.

# 3 REVELATION

The ride to church was somewhat painful since I sat with a total stranger while Delilah was seated next to Charisse and talked her to death about everything under the sun. I didn't even remember them talking about church but rather chatting away about stuff Charisse was supposed to talk about with me. I had to act like I didn't care and I wasn't sure if I really did or not.

What I thought would be a one hour bus ride turned out to be twice as long. It gave my mind too much time to wander. I noticed Chuck was in the front of the bus talking to some girl. He seemed to talk to her with the same verve he had when he talked with me, and that made me begin to hate him like I began to hate everyone else on that bus. I hated Delilah for taking over my invitation to Charisse, Charisse for talking to Delilah and not having said two words to me the whole time, at Chuck for talking to that girl the same way he talked to me, and at everyone else for ignoring the fact that I had no one to talk to.

As my mind continued to wander, I began to feel that familiar feeling. I smelled the fetid scent of gunpowder and heard the chamber of a revolver spinning like it was playing Russian Roulette with itself. It finally stopped, then I heard several clicks. When it got to the last click, I knew the gun was about to go off because all of the empty chambers had been exhausted. My heart began to race as I knew it was about to shoot, and I had the feeling that bullet was a special one that had enough force to kill everybody up in that bus. Then a strange thing happened; the gun changed position and before I knew it, it was pointed at me! When the trigger was finally pulled, a woman in white jumped in front of it and took the bullet for me. Instead of bleeding, nothing but beams of light came out of her body. Then the light turned into what looked like angels in military gear. They began to swarm me as they rapidly flapped their wings until I was lifted up off the ground. I got so high in the sky that I wound up sitting on a cloud and looked down at everyone. I realized all the people I was looking at wore the same clothes that I did. Then when I focused even more, they had on the same clothes I had on. When I focused again, they even had my face! One me was talking to Charisse, another me was talking to Delilah, and another me was at the front of the bus talking to some girl. I even saw a fourth me standing on line in the student cafeteria with her back turned to the world.

"No weapon that is formed against you shall prosper!" I heard a person say, which shook me out of my mind. At first I thought the person was talking to me after having read my mind, but I realized a conversation was going on about how Christians have God's protection and that nothing anyone ever says or does will ever prevail unless God says so. It seemed those Christians were so powerful that they were able to unwittingly stop four mental murders with a gun that never failed me. I did not know who the woman was who jumped in front of me, but I suspected it was the same one who did so when I would dream about Madame Samedie. I remembered what the pastor said about Michael the Archangel who fights heavenly battles and the angelic soldiers who are part of his army. But what I didn't understand why, when I got high in the sky and was at the point where I could clearly see everything, everyone I was mad with looked like *me*.

Before I had a chance to do any further decoding, the bus had already pulled up to the church. I slowly rose out of my seat and was somewhat nervous about entering a real religious setting without Mari for the first time. There was no familiar campus or a strictly student population. The church consisted of families and people in black suits with white collars. The other part of my nervousness was due to the fact that I felt invisible. I wasn't sure if I should have walked ahead or waited for Delilah and Charisse, who both seemed to be doing fine without me. Then there was Chuck at the front still talking his head off like what he had to say was so interesting. I could see his eyes dancing as he talked and I tried not to stare so much before I got caught. I would have to pass him and muster up a greeting without showing my displeasure. The entire time we were on the bus, not once did he look back to see if I was there.

The time came when it was my turn to file out. I stepped off the bus and walked as slowly as I could hoping Delilah would race behind me and tell me to wait up, but she didn't. She and Charisse were still engrossed in their own conversation, clearly forgetting I was the one who made the decision to invite Charisse in the first place. Fortunately I was interrupted by one of the people who was part of the group I sat with in the cafeteria.

"Hey! I remember you! So glad you could come join us."

His name was Mark and he seemed really friendly. I was hoping he'd keep talking to me so I could follow him into the church and have someone to sit with, but he just smiled and walked ahead to catch up with whomever he planned to sit beside.

Once we got inside, everyone was smiling, hugging, shaking hands and making emphatic small talk. There was another group of what looked like college kids and everyone seemed to know the people who rode on the bus from my college. All of that smiling and hugging, and no one noticed I was walking by myself and obviously didn't know where I was going or what I was doing. I felt like going back to the bus, but instead I just stood by the wall in the vestibule area with my arms folded. At some point someone would realize I was mad and finally talk to me long enough to relieve me of my awkward feelings. As far as I knew I had no problem with God, but my problem with Christians was coming back.

"Hey Suzi! Come sit with me." It was Chuck. I still pretended to be mad, but inside I was fluttering like a butterfly. I had never felt that way before and I acted reluctant because I could not process my feelings properly. I didn't even know him that well and he wasn't my type. But there was something about him that made me feel funny—so funny that I loved and hated the feeling at the same time. I hated that he acted like everything was alright and didn't notice I was mad. He should have figured out I was mad at him for not talking to me. It was all over my face. Apparently he, like all the other Christians, seemed to be impervious to bad attitudes and countenances.

I was hoping we would not sit near the front, but we wound up almost front and center. And not only that, we were sitting with a bunch of talkative college girls who treated Chuck like a rock star. It made me feel special to be sitting next to him at his request, so I took special care to turn my nose up at the girls who tried to talk to him yet didn't speak to me. I then became more preoccupied with how it was the third time Chuck grabbed a hold of me. The logical side of me figured since I was new to this Christian thing, he wanted to make sure I was hanging in there. However, the emotional side of me wanted to believe he liked me. More than likely it was the former reason, but if I could daydream about all kinds of crazy stuff, I could do so with something good for a change. I would dream even if, as my mother would have me believe, it wasn't worth hoping for.

After a while I began to forget all that I thought about on the way to church and began to drift away into a more beautiful place. The butterflies were still flying around inside of me, and extremely restless because not one time did they set their feet on the ground. I couldn't pay attention to the people singing, the person making the announcements, and all the other stuff going on around me. I was somewhere in the park having a picnic with Chuck. We were on a checkered blanket with our initials sewn in each one. We laughed and joked and talked about how wrong my mother was for keeping me from loving someone. I told him that he was the best thing that ever happened to me. Then after that, we were in the mall shopping together and my nose was back in the air because those same girls wanted his attention, yet I was the one who got it. Next we dropped in the jewelry store and were looking at wedding rings. In a flash we were at the altar and about to be pronounced man and wife when suddenly someone in the back stood up and began hurling threats at us. Her hair was wild and gray, and she had so much that it covered her face. She was rocking from side to side trying to get the ushers to let go of her. When she finally broke free, she began running towards me with her arms outstretched, opening and closing her hands as though she was eager to touch me in the way my mother said a sopper would touch people to steal their gifts. As soon as she got close to me, Chuck grabbed her by the wrist and said, "It's too late!"

I was curious and tried to brush the woman's hair away from her face to see who she was, which made Chuck scream, "Suzi no!" But it was too late. I had already made contact. And when our eyes met, I began to cry rose water tears as she said tersely, "Good morning, *motherless child.*"

The thought jolted me back into reality and I was just in time to hear Pastor Michael say, "But God can break the curse! The Bible says God's Word does not return void. And I'd like to add that the words others have spoken over your life cannot trump what God has ordained. Let every man be a liar, but let God be true!"

No sooner had he said "true", it felt like an electric shock ran through me and I jumped out of my seat as though I were on fire. I shook my hands trying to drop the imaginary hot potato that came out of nowhere. Some ladies from the front row rushed to me and led me out into the aisle where I kept jumping up and down. I began stammering and I found myself speaking in tongues again. That time I was speaking harshly like a mother who was reprimanding a child.

"Let her go! Let her go!" I heard Pastor Michael say. "Let her go! Satan, the blood of Jesus Christ is against you!"

I was sufficiently embarrassed yet at the same time I was happy to not be in control of myself. All of the negative energy I had built up from the bus ride was being released and I wanted to hear more of what Pastor Michael would say to me to help me understand myself. By the time I had calmed down, I began to hear other people crying and feet moving rapidly. Some people were rushing to the front of the church throwing money on the steps to the pulpit, while others fell to their knees, threw their heads back, and began talking to God—some in tongues and others in English. I saw Charisse and Delilah at the altar. One was praying and one was crying for dear life begging God to please don't let her die.

The ladies who tended to me when I was on fire sat me down and began to fan me. One of them, who looked old enough to be my grandmother, began to sing as she fanned me. She kept wiping my face with a white handkerchief that felt like it had been soaked in oil. She took my face in both her hands and kissed me on my forehead, and she smiled at me like she knew me and all that I was about. She has a familiar look in her eyes as though I looked into them every night from the day I was born.

Almost two hours had passed from the time I got rid of the imaginary potato to the time the church began to clear out. Only a few of us were left behind, including the church lady who fanned me and gave me sweet kisses. She was sitting at the end of the pew fanning herself and humming the same tune she hummed when she wiped me down with oil. She rocked from side to side while tapping her small feet to a tune that was only playing in her head. She watched Charisse as she was being prayed for by Pastor Michael, then turned to me as if she could read my thoughts and answered a question I hadn't yet thought to ask.

"I'm Mother Tibideau, Pastor Michael's great aunt. Pleased to finally meet you, Blessed Child. Yes indeed."

"Yes indeed" was all she had to say and I knew her story just as well as she knew mine. She had an accent that reminded me of my mother's when she got really mad, and a fleur de lis pin on the collar of her blouse. It all began to make sense. *Too much sense.* I had heard of coincidences and fate, but things were happening so exact that I began to feel terrified about what it all meant. I wanted Mother Tibideau to say more, but she just looked at me and smiled. She seemed the type to not say more than she was supposed to and that she would go to the grave with secrets and mysteries only reserved for people who wore white. She left me to my thoughts knowing at some point I would catch on. It then made sense why Pastor Michael had a look of acknowledgment when I told him my family name. Somehow his family knew mine and I began to feel that relationship was an antagonistic one— antagonistic enough to give my grandmother gray hairs and thoughts of cursing my mother's womb. It was also enough to put me in the presence of a person who could tell me about me before I was born and about being the seed who would destroy the line.

I turned my attention to Charisse who was still stretched out on the floor like she was praying to the ground. She was still crying and asking God "Why?" in between wails. Charisse was the biggest drama queen I had ever seen. It was just like her to suck up all the air in the room. I kept watching Pastor Michael as he worked with her and hoped he'd give her a detailed message about herself. It was time Charisse knew how messed up she was. Someone she didn't know had to point out to her things I had been telling her all along—things that cost me my reputation for remaining her friend even though I didn't do the things she did. If it wasn't for her, half the campus wouldn't believe I was someone I wasn't. But out of loyalty to our friendship and the belief that people wouldn't accuse me of things they never actually saw me do, I stayed by her side to defend her when people tried to spread rumors that caused me to constantly pull her out of dorm rooms. I was frequently hit with so many bad things that came with our friendship and half the time I questioned who was really benefitting. Thinking about it made me realize what a burden she was to me and that I couldn't move on with my life in a positive direction with her around. Looking at her lying on the floor made me sick.

While Charisse was still on the floor a weepin' and a wailin', Pastor Michael began whispering in her ear. Every few moments Charisse would nod then let out a cry even louder than the last one. I heard him tell her to calm down and focus, and something about accepting what happened and taking responsibility for moving on. He cautioned her to not destroy herself because someone else tried to. I knew he had to be speaking of her father, Two Tufts Jones, as my mother called him during the pre-voodoo doll clown days. It seemed like forever when Charisse came off the altar and finally dried her eyes. Mother Tibideau called her over and gave her a huge hug, which made Charisse cry all over again. All I could do was roll my eyes; she was getting way too much sympathy. The Charisse Show was in full effect.

While I continued to loathe Charisse, Mother Tibideau gave me a knowing look, then threw her white handkerchief to me and said, "Wipe your eyes, child." Without a second thought I wiped my eyes thinking I was still crying and didn't know it.

"Can you see now?" she asked me.

"See what?"

"Yourself."

I wanted to understand what Mother Tibideau said to me, but I was too overwhelmed with my own confusing thoughts of the day. I didn't want to go back to campus, but I didn't want to stay in church either.

"Child, I want you and your friends to come by my house for dinner, hear? I have some good food for your soul. You like spicy? You like jambalaya, dirty rice, you know, that real good food?" Mother Tibideau asked.

"Thank you, but I'm not ready yet," I quickly blurted out as though I knew I would be invited at a later date. Taking for granted the forgiving nature Christians were supposed to have, I didn't think twice about how Mother Tibideau would take my tacit response. She appeared as though she was about to insist, but changed her mind to accommodate the look of fear on my face. She signaled to Pastor Michael to come over and whispered something to him, while I stayed in my seat wiping tears that had worn grooves into my face. I was so overwhelmed by all of the emotion and attention that the only way to express it was to cry a river. The only drawback was that there were too many people paddling around in it; I wanted to go home.

Same as it happened during the campus Bible study, people began to file out once the altar began to clear. People seemed to like to linger around, which struck me as strange. When I went to church with Mari, people left after the benediction. They said their hellos and goodbyes but did not hang around until the lights went off. Delilah's Christians were a different breed to me. They seemed as though they didn't like to go home and were always running to the front of the church looking to be saved again or something. They acted like dependents as though if someone were not around to give them huge amounts of spiritual attention, they wouldn't make it. I wasn't sure if that spiritual reality was for me, but I had to admit the attention I had received being involved with Delilah was much needed, albeit unwanted. My contradictory emotions reminded me of an argument I had with Mari.

"You know you probably don't want to admit it, but you have a problem making up your mind."

As usual, I would contest Mari's observations of me and her charges of me with not being more like her.

"You are always very conflicted," she continued. "It's like yes, no, maybe, who cares. Make a choice!"

"Unlike yourself, my choices are to please me, which gives me the freedom to change my mind a million times. You? You make choices for other people so that you can keep up appearances and feel good about yourself. So which one of us is *really* conflicted?"

While Mari was no punk, she knew to back down when I was ready to stick a pin in her eye. Most times I would let her get away with her diatribes, and then there were times she would catch me after I calculated the weight of all the stones I could throw at her. If I were a different kind of person, she would have been stoned to death. But like everything else, I couldn't make up my mind if I wanted to be her friend or enemy in that moment, and decided to grind my weapons of emotional destruction to powder.

Our arguments would always end in silence. If I had someplace to go, I would storm out and Mari wouldn't blink. If I didn't, I'd resume whatever I was doing and so would Mari. The next time we spoke it'd be as though nothing happened. But as with everything in my life, nothing was ever what it seemed. As I recalled those memories, I began to see how Mari would experience the wear and tear of training me in the way that I should go, and me taking her strength for granted would not let me think twice about not fixing some things to make our friendship flow. But as the truth would have it, there were some things I was tired of as well and maybe my need for the stability she gave me caused me to overlook those things.

I had begun to wish that I was ignorant of all the things I

experienced and saw since deciding I would dip my toe in the pool of religion. I had no idea someone would come behind me and push me in the water and expect me to swim. I felt like I would never be able to touch the sides ever again and would have to learn how to float without ceasing in order to survive.

"Yes," I replied before I realized it came out of my mouth.

"It's settled then. Michael, you drive my car and carry these girls with you. Take it back to campus and bring it back to me next time you come down. Make haste, okay?"

Pastor Michael just waved his hand in acknowledgment as he continued to work with other people who wanted prayer. I figured by the time he would be done, the food would probably get cold even if the fire was still under them. Church people didn't know when to stop praying.

Eventually we made it to Mother Tibideau' house, which to my surprise was more modern than I had expected. It had a circular driveway, impeccable landscaping, and a white Cadillac parked in front with personalized plates that read HOLY77. I thought how she must be big time because we rode in her second car of the same make but different model, with plates that read JESUS77. As we entered the house, it was obvious a church person lived there. We were greeted by a chorus of angels as we entered the foyer. Mother Tibideau said she always left music playing over the intercom to keep the presence of God in the house, and that anyone who entered couldn't help but keep their mind on the Lord. As we went further into the house, she showed us to the sitting room where all of the furniture was white with soft pink pillows in different designs. The furniture was cherry wood with intricate carvings on the arms and legs. Fresh flowers seemed to be everywhere, which matched the various shades found in the pillows.

Charisse eyeballed every part of the room and walked around like a tourist as she dragged her hands over everything. She acted as though she had never been anywhere, but then I had to remember the state of her household and how uncomfortable it was; junky inside and out. Her lack of home training didn't allow her to think she was supposed to come in and sit down, and not touch all over people's stuff.

"Charisse! Charisse!" I whispered loudly as I tried to get her to sit down and stop embarrassing herself. She just ignored me then starting saying random stuff.

"This is nice! This must cost a lot!"

"Charisse, don't say that!" I scolded. "That's people's business!"

She gave me an "I wasn't talking to you" look then finally sat down as Mother Tibideau just smiled, cosigning that Charisse needed to shut up and sit down like I was trying to tell her.

"Oh, this stuff isn't expensive. At least not when I bought it. See, I had this for years. They made good furniture back then. Everything was sturdy and built to last. Nowadays people just want shiny stuff—temporary things to impress people that don't mean nothing to them. The more time passes the more temporary things become, seem like."

We were told to make ourselves comfortable while Mother Tibideau went into the kitchen and prepared the food. By that time Pastor Michael had disappeared through a sliding glass door that led to another part of the house. Mother Tibideau had Cadillacs, old school sturdy furniture, and a sunroom. That lady was living large.

I turned my head to look through the doors to see who Pastor Michael was talking to. It was Chuck, who had been dropped off before us. I soon came to learn that Chuck was very close to Pastor Michael and often stayed with Mother Tibideau instead of going all the way back to Tennessee on holiday weekends. He even had his own room and use of the third car, which was in the garage. I made a bet that those license plates had sevens it in it too, only to find I was right. By that time I wanted to be like Charisse and start asking questions. I wondered if Mother Tibideau used to be a preacher or something and bought all those things with church money.

Chuck and Pastor Michael finally came inside the house and led Delilah, Charisse, and me into the dining area. There were two other ladies there helping to serve the food that looked like they were in their sixties like Mother Tibideau. They smiled at me and I began to feel there was a joke going on where I would be the last to laugh. Mother introduced them as Sally and Minnie Lee, her two sisters visiting from South Carolina. Whenever Pastor Michael preached at the country church, they would fly in to support him.

"He's our baby!" Minnie Lee said. "He makes the family proud. A pastor in the family!"

"Bishop even!" Sally chimed in.

They had thick accents, a mix of Cajun country and Gullah. Had my mother not shared their heritage, I would not have understood a word they said. They talked so fast that is sounded as though they spoke another language. And their voices were heavy like they spoke from their feet. They were robust women who looked like they've seen a lot of things—things that they shared only amongst themselves. When the food finally arrived, Sally gave the prayer.

"Father, oh Holy Father! We come before you thanking you for this day, this meal, and these souls…"

"HOLY GHOST AND FIRE! POWER LORD!" Minnie Lee rang out.

"We thank you for always taking care of us and taking us…"
"HIGHER! YES LORD!"

"And we ask you to make the food nourishing for our bodies, let it continue to multiply in thy…"

"HOLY!"

"…cupboard and bless us to keep blessing you. In Jesus'…"

"THE HOLY ONE OF IS-RA-EL!!! YES CHILDREN! CRY OUT HOLY!"

"…name, amen."

Pastor Michael and Chuck began to hee haw like little school kids, as did everyone else except Charisse and me. I didn't see anything funny about Minnie Lee with the maxi voice scaring the dickens out of us. When I glanced at Charisse, she looked like she was about to choke on imaginary food. I heard her knee bang against the table and the silverware scramble to get out of the way when she jumped at the first HOLY. If the table wasn't in the way, Charisse would have been on the ceiling hanging on by the nails of her hands and feet like a cat who was frightened out of its fur. The thought made me giggle thinking had it been her father, there'd be two tufts on the floor.

Minnie Lee and Sally were going back and forth taking turns saying, "Yes, umm hmm" to each other. They acted like they lived together, which I learned they did. From the way they behaved at the table— speaking in tandem throughout the dinner and nodding at each other like they had to touch antennae for every thought—was the weirdest thing I had ever seen. They were even tasting each other's food as though they couldn't get a sample from the many dishes on the table. With each bite they'd look at each other and say, "Yes umm hmm" or an emphatic "Yes, very fresh! Indeed!" It seemed like they had been in each other's world with no outside influences for too long. It was time for them to break up.

Everyone seemed to be in their own world and I had hoped it stayed that way, but Mother Tibideau had this way of seeing through a person down to the slip. Even when her attention was elsewhere, I felt my nerves were exposed to her spiritual touch. I reluctantly began to anticipate her saying something to me. I wanted her to say anything to remind me that I mattered at that moment. But it seemed no one noticed soon enough that I was quiet, probably because Charisse talked between mouthfuls and asked a lot of questions, paid compliments about trivial things like the buttons on Minnie Lee's dress, or the lace chaplets Sally wore because, as she explained, the Bible said a woman must have her head covered when she prays.

Mother Tibideau glanced at me while I ate and asked if I wanted more. She was offering me food but after "more" I filled in the blank. I wanted more of whatever it would take for me to not feel like a stranger amongst people who showed themselves friendly. I wanted more of whatever Minnie Lee and Sally had that made them be in each other's company as though for the first time, even though they lived together. I wanted more of what Chuck and Pastor Michael had as they sat outside talking on the sun porch earlier that evening like old friends who were broken in like a favorite pair of house slippers. And I couldn't take it anymore.

"Where is the bathroom?" I asked, hoping it wasn't too far because my tears were about to ask for directions themselves. I was pointed to a corridor that took me away from the dining room and deeper into the house. I became distracted by the open bedroom doors and decided to take a peek. The room was neatly kept and it looked like it would be a room in a dollhouse with the huge antique clock, lace bedspread, and light colors with flowering borders on almost everything. The wood was a dark cherry wood that reminded me of the furniture in my bedroom, except what I was missing in mine was found in that room. Hearing the talking grow louder in the dining room, I became lost in a maze of pictures without fear of discovery. I had hoped everyone would forget I was gone or think I "fell in" and would swim my way out and empty into the sunroom to dry out.

There was one album in particular that was already sticking out of the pile as though someone had recently looked through it and didn't put it back. I dared to open it and found old pictures of Mother Tibideau, her sisters, and other family members. The album looked like it was telling a visual story from childhood to adulthood. Mother Tibideau apparently had three sisters, one of which seemed to be like, yet unlike, the rest of the sisters. When Mother Tibideau, Minnie Lee, and Sally stood together, the fourth one would stand a little apart as though she didn't want to be in the picture. I was eager to find out who that person was who was so unlike the three and if she was still alive. As I correctly guessed, she had to be the youngest as the first page with the solo picture was of the eldest, Mother Tibideau, then Sally, then Minnie Lee, who was Sally's fraternal twin and younger by seven minutes according to the caption. When I got to the fourth sister, the acknowledgment of her adult face made the hair on the back of my neck stand up as the book slammed closed on its own and my vocal chords stretched to give the loudest, most blood-curdling scream my body had ever heard or given.

"It's time to deal with it," I heard Mother Tibideau say. "It's time."

I ran out of the house at full speed, not even pausing to make sure I didn't bump anyone's chair as I zipped through the dining room. I felt like I was on the verge of a breakdown having seen my grandmother's picture in a stranger's photo album; a stranger who was the sister of my grandmother whom I thought had no siblings or any origins at all. My mother kept every living relative away from me—citing they were all either dead or crazy—leaving just the two of us, Reesie, and Camille, the eldest sister we rarely saw. I had no contact with my father's family as my mother made sure she somehow he remained at a distance.

Because I didn't know where I was, by the time I reached the edge of the front lawn I had come to a complete stop and bent over in full agony. I was in too much pain to wag my finger at God for springing so much on me after only two days of Christianity in my life. Even with my limited knowledge of how things worked in the religion, no one could convince me that what I was experiencing was the way things were really done. By the time I came back to myself, Chuck had me by the shoulders, turned me around, and gave me a comforting embrace. At that point I almost forgot about my grandmother and melted into his arms. A warm current that only happens in spring washed over me and my heart was beating faster than a hummingbird's. I was glad I had a moment of fright so that I would not give myself away to Chuck. I didn't want to reveal that I was excited because of him and not because of what I had seen.

As Chuck held me, I could smell the fresh cut grass and hear the lawn sprinklers pivoting back and forth in the well-manicured yards on Mother Tibideau's block. The sound of the drops of water frolicking amongst the blades of grass like they were sliding boards made me feel as though I was being watered with a bunch of things. I didn't want the moment to end, but I didn't want to exaggerate what it meant. For Chuck it was just a means to comfort his newfound sister in the Lord. For me, it was a chance to feel human.

The others stood on the lawn watching us as though we were in a movie and one of us was about to say goodbye forever. One by one everyone began to file back in as Chuck slowly led me back to the house.

"Let's walk please," I urged. "I'm not ready yet."

Chuck signaled to everyone that we'd be in later. Mother Tibideau nodded the kind of nod that said if she says yes, you go, and if she says no, you stay. We continued to walk and my warm current dwindled to a tepid stream as Chuck released me from his grip and walked with his hands behind his back. I placed my hands in my pockets, both fists balled up in that familiar position that meant I wanted to hurt somebody. Chuck was the first to speak.

"Are you okay?"

I really wasn't as I vacillated between confusing feelings of the joy of Chuck's attention and the confusion of finding out the dead had arisen. I didn't know what to feel as I spent a good portion of my life detached from what was normal and attached to nothing but smoke and mirrors. Half the time I wasn't sure if I was even real. I would sometimes look in the mirror and frighten myself because I could not believe I was looking at something living. I used to say to myself "I'm alive!", which would send me into a tailspin of thoughts challenging my existence and wondering if the person I was looking at was also looking at me, too. Then I'd snap back to reality and tell myself I was experiencing a "don't try this at home" moment.

Chuck reminded me once again of my existence and asked me to tell him about myself from beginning to end. Apparently we had all the time in the world, even though I didn't need it as I no longer knew who I was, where I came from, and where I was even going.

I began the way I always did by starting with my single mother in the house, my father who was away somewhere in West Virginia, and who I knew somehow loved me but was more afraid of my mother than the repercussions of not being a father to me. I really didn't care because he was not in my life long enough for me to bond with him since my mother always made it clear I only had one parent. Chuck then began to ask me more specific questions as he saw everything I said was more on the surface, but he did not realize I was not accustomed to scratching it. I was too busy being angry and tormented by what I now know was my mother's dealings with witchcraft. She thought she was protecting me, but the reality showed that she was really exposing me to all of the things that would try to destroy me. What I could not understand was the rapid pace of my introduction to Christianity.

"God is doing what we call a blitz," Chuck answered.

"A what?"

"A blitz. Suzi, your case is pretty extreme so God had to do an immediate deliverance on you. It's no accident you are surrounded by mature Christians who are experienced in that kind of ministry."

"But even so, the average person could not experience all the stuff I did in so short a time and not lose their mind."

"True, but you are a different case. You were exposed to things like this all along and you somehow found a way to deny it. These things are not new for you, but you finally acknowledging their reality is new. That's the difference between you and the average Christian; most Christians don't even realize the spirit realm exists."

Chuck continued by explaining there were two realms; the spirit realm and the natural realm. The spirit realm was the unseen and the natural dealt with the seen. Most Christians believed in the seen and chose to leave whatever mysteries there were in the faith to the priests and pastors. Chuck practiced a brand of Christianity that taught all Christians had access to the mysteries of God and had power over evil. Despite most people not believing in the power of the devil, he said if we can believe God can bless, we should equally be able to believe that the devil can curse. There was no such thing as if you don't believe in evil and curses that they won't work. Evil operates independent of faith and dependent on willful ignorance of its power.

We talked more about what I experienced growing up as I was relieved that I had a safe place to divulge the things I tucked away for so long. There was something about Chuck that was like a truth serum. I needed the intimacy and safety that a sincere listening ear offered. It just felt right. When I thought I was sufficiently purged of what I was willing to divulge about my home life, Chuck asked me about my friendships and how he thought it strange I was friends with Charisse based on things he'd heard about her, and also strange that I was friends with Mari because she had an opposite demeanor. I began to clam up when he mentioned Mari's name and suggested we go back to the house.

"Sorry. I didn't realize I hit a sore spot," Chuck apologized.

"You couldn't miss it if you were blindfolded. Apparently I'm sore all over."

I sabotaged the moment I needed because of a person who no longer wanted me in her life. I didn't want to make Mari's problem with me into a problem with Chuck, so I tried to find a way to apologize without bringing attention to the fact that I imposed upon him a bipolar conversation.

"It's okay, Suzi. We are just getting to know each other and, you know, I got so comfortable learning about you. I find you interesting and I think I understand you. I hope we have more conversations like this and you can ask me whatever you want. I'm an open book."

Without saying a word, I looked into his face and nodded my head. I felt both sides of my mind were fighting the moment because letting myself go was not something I ever did, but I guess the new little voice in my head was telling me to turn old Suzi loose to fend for herself and let the new one emerge.

When we arrived at the house, Charisse was bolting out of the door and coming out of her clothes and asking God a rhetorical question while Delilah had the sleeves of Charisse's sweater, which were empty of arms. My eyes rolled far back into my head as I just knew Charisse couldn't stand for me to have a moment. I imagined if my mother were there, she'd casually order someone to "Tell that nut to shut up!"

Mother Tibideau stood in the door and hollered, "Everybody back in the house! My God!", followed by an "Ooh, Lord! I can't. I just can't! This generation...JESUS! The blood, Sir! The blood!"

We took a seat in the living room where there apparently would be a pow wow. The twins were mumbling to themselves really fast, "Yea yea yea yea! Mmmmmm, glory. Yes suh. Glory glory glory glory. Thank ya. Mmmmm, shata. Yea yea yea yea!"

"Michael, what happened in here?" Chuck whispered.

Pastor Michael gave Chuck a "pauvricita" look and turned his head so Mother Tibideau wouldn't catch him divulging before the time. She made Delilah take Charisse into another room to calm down. Apparently the living room pow wow was for me.

"Suzi, the time has come for you to know the truth about yourself and your family." Mother Tibideau began by explaining that she and her sister were indeed my great aunts and that Pastor Michael was my half brother.

"What?!" I screamed.

As Mother Tibideau continued, I learned that she and her sisters were the women who would come to my grandmother's house and pray over her, and even made the prophetic pronouncement about the seed destroying the line. Pastor Michael was my mother's first born—the one who was prophesied to destroy my grandmother's wicked line and the one who my grandmother said would be a motherless child. When he was born, my mother put him up for adoption in order to nullify the prophecy. To ensure he would never find her, she stipulated that the adopting parents had to be out of the state and would never have access to the birth family's information. This opened the door for Mother Tibideau and her late husband, John, to adopt him without my mother knowing because, by that time, she had left New York and returned to the South. She never kept in contact with my mother because of my mother's desire to continue the practices of my grandmother.

"Your grandmother was a powerful Seer. Very powerful," Mother Tibideau explained. "But what happened to her happened to so many people in the  church. People saw her gift and started to elevate her and push her into ministry too soon. You can't do God's work unless God has done a work!"

"Amen!" the twins chimed.

"Without the fruit of the Spirit, the gifts of the Spirit are perverted. Anyone in a leadership position who does not have a humble spirit, tries to control everything, and is never wrong is a witch in training. Your grandmother did not develop the fruit of meekness, which opened the door to pride and led to her deception. The devil took her out of the kingdom of God for good, even when she was still in the church. The dead were amongst the living and killing folk all the while."

Mother Tibideau recalled a story when my grandmother was at the height of her gifting in the church. She remembered how my grandmother used to travel with their pastor to different churches to perform deliverance services. She was what was called an armor bearer— a person who made sure the pastor was protected spiritually and had someone to watch the congregation for witches. Although she was there to watch for the pastor, there were people watching for her because they knew she had a powerful gift of prophecy. People would form long lines to be prayed for and when they got to the front, they would whisper to the pastor to let my grandmother pray for them. Soon my grandmother began to believe her own press and elevated herself above the leadership in her church. It got to the point where she accused her own pastor of holding her back from spiritual greatness.

"They are scared of me and my power," my grandmother said to Mother Tibideau the day she left the church.

"You better be careful, Augustine. You can't trump your own pastor. When you start thinking like that, you are full of pride and you either have to fall in line or leave."

"You see those people line up whenever I'm at the service? God is doing a new thing and the pastor don't want to step aside. He's holding me back."

Mother Tibideau pleaded with her older, more gifted sister. She pleaded with the fervor of the woman in the Bible who begged that her child be given to the false claimant lest it be ripped in two to settle the dispute.

"Augustine, it's not your power; it's God's power. Don't let those people make a star out of you. Pastor is not trying to hold you back; he's trying to save your soul from being taken over by another spirit. I see the door is open. Don't let it walk in."

Young Augustine did not listen and she was soon asked to leave the church when the pastor realized she would not submit to leadership. She was told not to prophesy to members because the church did not want to be held responsible for her words, true or not. However, my grandmother would still boldly minister to members of the congregation without the pastor's permission. That was the last straw and the leadership voted to have her ousted. It was as though she had the mark of the beast or something because other churches in her small parish would not allow her to attend. She was a woman who would not submit, and she dared to minister at a time when women were only allowed to pray and give the announcements.

It was not until Augustine left Louisiana for New York with a bitter heart that she was able to reinvent herself with a new set of eager congregants and took up her ways again. She began holding her own services out of her home and telling people what they wanted to hear. While her prophecies came to pass, people began to believe they weren't from God when things would go wrong soon after her words came to pass. The remedy was to tell them that they didn't have enough faith or would have to supplement the prophecy by listening to other spirits that knew just as much as God.

"Listen, there are some things God will not tell you because he thinks you can't handle it," my grandmother said to a couple who was contemplating going into full-time ministry. "Sometimes you have to go another route."

"But isn't it the devil when it doesn't come from God?" the woman asked with a concerned sound in her voice.

"See, the church makes you believe everything is black and white. It is not always God talking. Sometimes it's an angel and those angels talk to me. They are from God."

"Like Gabriel?" the husband, Minister Herman, asked.

"That's right. He's the messenger angel."

"Honey, I don't know about this," the wife interjected. She was the only voice of reason in the room.

Prophetess Augustine proceeded to explain that sometimes people have to prove to God they can handle information, so at times he will allow a "lesser spirit" to tell them things in order to prep them for God's official message. All she needed was $100 from them and some hair from the husband.

"What do you need his hair for?" the voice of reason queried.

"That man is going into ministry! If he wants the strength of Samson, I need his hair. Let me pull it."

Prophetess Augustine ran her fingers through the aspiring pastor's coif and pulled out a few strands of shed coils. When she proceeded to ask for the money, the voice of reason interrupted again. Instead of my grandmother answering her back, she looked at the husband with a serious look and told him to come close so that she could whisper in his ear. She lulled Minister Herman into an almost dream-like state, she had whispered for so long. When she was done, the pastor-to-be looked at his wife with righteous indignation, got up, and left her in the room. She ran behind him screaming, "What did she say? What did she say?"

Soon after, the couple had gotten a divorce and Minister Herman, who soon became Pastor Herman, started his church with a new wife who was not American in order to attract an international congregation. The ministry struggled from its inception and at first he wanted to blame it on attacks of the devil, then he figured there was someone inside the congregation who was a weapon formed against it. After scapegoating people who didn't tell him what he wanted to hear, and subsequently banning them from the church, he thought he had gotten rid of the problem. All ears perked when a respected prophet visited the church and ministered to the well-deceived pastor about the root of the problem. What the struggling pastor had done wrong was listen to someone with a familiar spirit tell him what his flesh wanted to hear, which was that he was ready for ministry and anyone who said otherwise was being used by the devil to hold him back. This included his former senior pastor, who became an enemy once he uttered the word "Wait." The over eager young pastor was also told that his wife was not God's first choice for him and she would hinder his ministry, when the reality was she was the right woman for him and was the key to the ministry's success.

Pastor Herman could not deny that around the time he thought he was ready for ministry was the same time he realized he was no longer attracted to his wife. As a result, it opened a door in his heart for him to lust after something that wasn't real. He saw other preachers with trophy wives and felt had he known he had a great calling before he had gotten holy sanctified, he would have married a trophy too. His discontent made him a prime candidate to be seduced with thoughts of divorcing his faithful wife. The prophet even told Pastor Herman that when Prophetess Augustine whispered in his ear, the spirit that was on her had infiltrated his mind to lull him into a spiritual sleep. That spirit distorted reality and caused him to embrace the false and reject the real. Reason, deduction, and wisdom were no longer his companions, and his ego served him a colder dish than revenge.

Pastor Herman didn't want to believe what he heard, but he could not deny the prophet's accuracy and great detail. The next time anyone saw him, he was renting a room in a moldy basement. His new wife left him after she received her citizenship, and the old wife, he learned, was somewhere in California married to a pastor of a mega church. And to boot, she was a size 6 and had work done on her teeth and skin. The man was another victim of being told a half-truth at the right time—and the truth at the wrong time—which caused him to step out too soon and crash just like Augustine.

"Too much too soon," Mother Tibideau said. "You can tell people the right thing at the wrong time and ruin their lives. By the time your grandmother passed away, there was not a person in town who did not believe what she did was the devil. It was outsiders who came to hear her speak. She had to get out of town, and that's how the branches of our tree spread out to New York. There are churches on every corner in that place. It was fertile ground for a fortune seeker in the name of the Lord."

Mother Tibideau continued her story about the colorful legacy by telling me the story about Michael's birth. After my mother bore Michael, she had a ritual performed on her to make sure there would never be a second opportunity for any seed to destroy anything.

"If you do this your womb will dry out. Never again will you yield a harvest from any seed planted in you," the priest said. "Here. Drink this, s'il vous plaît."

My mother drank a concoction that made her feel like her insides were committing suicide. She ran around the room in circles screaming that she just killed herself. Her eyes rolled backward and she fell into a trance, babbling something about a child who would walk amongst the living. The priest stood back and shook his head in resignation.

"It won't work," he whispered to another initiate. "It won't work. The fate of her womb has been set in stone. I cannot undo it, but I will not tell her. If I tell her now, she will set herself on fire to stop the prophecy."

"But what can she do? The child must not be born," the initiate declared.

"The child will be born. She cannot take the child's body, but she will try to kill her spirit by making her dead to life. But that too will not work. *C'est difficile*. There have been prayers that have gone out over the child that, in due season, will undo all that we attempt to do now. We must wash our hands and let her go. I do not want that power to come back and destroy us."

"What power is that?"

"The Holy Ghost. Our deepest medicine will not work. We must wash our hands."

"By the time your mother had you," Mother Tibideau continued, "she was more advanced in her practices and felt she could nullify any predictions on her own. That's when my sisters and I really began to fast and pray to keep your soul until the appointed time. God assigned me to you as your intercessor. That's why I looked familiar to you when you saw me. God would show you in dreams how I interceded for you whenever that priestess in Haiti tried to pull on your spirit. I was the one who would jump in front of her whenever she got close to you. Those were my prayers shielding you."

I let out a gasp that surprised everyone, including myself. The thought that someone who never knew me would pray for me, to the point where she'd come in my dreams to protect me, was a kind of love and care that I did not know existed. She explained the idea of intercessory prayer, which was when people prayed on behalf of others, and sometimes those who could not pray for themselves. Mother Tibideau had been praying for me my entire life. Even though I accepted Jesus Christ into my life and was on the path to learn to pray for myself, she said she would still pray for me because the battle would not be over until my mother accepted that she had to bow down at the name of Jesus.

Mother Tibideau continued that my mother designed my life to keep me open to being plagued. She omitted people from my life who had the potential to convert me to real Christianity and kept me in an unstable environment so that I would be emotionally and mentally stifled. My anger and lack of stability growing up created a ripe environment for The Blacksmith to remain active in my life. My mother had me damaged in almost every area in an attempt to make me detached, distrustful of men, and insular. In order to offset this until I was ready to accept Him, God allowed Mari to come into my life to open me up to His existence due to her father being a minister, and he allowed Charisse to come into my life to create in me a space for compassion so that my heart would not grow so hard that I would never allow the truth to be planted in my heart. The two people I was closest to were then allowed to be ripped from me all at once so that I would feel I had nowhere to turn but to something bigger than myself. All of the events that took place on campus that day were part of some bigger plan to get me to accept Jesus into my life and be free from everything that had plagued me. I had to die to be born again. Even the fact that I got accepted into the college I attended, when my original plan was to remain in New York, was by divine design. Me, the very person who thought nothing I couldn't see was real, was under the influence of it the whole time, all the way down to where I stood at that moment hearing about my life.

"Honey, I have been praying for you before you were even born. I knew your mother would have another child. When Michael told me you came to the campus church that day and told me the family name, I knew God had brought this thing full circle. I had to see you with my own eyes. Baby, welcome home. You have a family now."

Everything began to make the most sense I have ever experienced in my entire life. I felt so much relief that my life and friendships were not the product of me having done something wrong, but that there was some special plan for me. At that moment I felt loved and cared for in a way I had never been able to feel.

With all of the puzzle pieces splayed before me, there was one more that I needed—to know what became of my grandmother. When I asked, Mother Tibideau looked away and began to tear up. Sally and Minnie Lee decided it was time to go to the dining room and clear the table. Pastor Michael and Chuck sensed that it was not going to be a good moment and decided to head to the sunroom. It took Mother Tibideau a moment before she decided to answer me. I knew there were more details that she may have felt it best for me to not know.

"Honey, all I will say is that…"

At that moment I noticed a light going off in my handbag. It was my pager that I had on silent. I asked Mother Tibideau if I could use her phone to contact my mother. She allowed me to do so, but I had to be sure to block the number first.

"Where in the hell are you?!" she screamed so loudly that Mother Tibideau heard her. I was not sure how to answer, so I decided to answer a question with a question.

"Why?"

My mother replied that she heard a commotion in my room and saw a large man standing over my bed with a flaming sword. When she looked him in the face, he lowered the sword, drew two parallel lines between them, and then stepped on them to break the lines in two.

"I'm gonna ask you one more time. Where in the devil's hell are you?"

Mother Tibideau immediately sprung to her feet and took the

phone from me.

"Esther, it's over."

I heard the banshee who was once my mother scream, hurl threats, and curse God six ways to nowhere. Mother Tibideau just kept the phone to her ear and kept saying, "The blood of Jesus" under her breath. The last thing I heard was a wicked, high-pitched scream and an "I hate you!" full of venom and witch's brew. It was the kind of scream befitting the Greek tragic figure Medea who rode off into the sky in a flaming chariot with her two dead children whom she killed for spite. Mother Tibideau then began to speak above her breath, quoting scripture and telling my mother no weapon that was formed against me shall prosper, and that I belonged to God and there was nothing she could do about it. My mother said she would die and take me with her before she takes a loss to anyone, and her vocal cords proceeded to spew blood and bile in her holy aunt's ear. In the midst of the screaming, I heard loud noises as though my mother was going through the cupboards and closets to find something to fight with. I knew my mother was going into the basement and was about to do something that would lift the house off the ground.

"In the name of Jesus! Satan the Lord rebuke you!" Mother Tibideau commanded. I thought she was still on the phone with my mother when I realized she had her hand on my hands. I looked down and saw I was in mid reach for a silver candelabra and getting ready to swing away at God.

"Satan, she is free in the name of Jesus! No weapon that is formed against her shall prosper! Loose your hold on her now! She belongs to Jesus!"

More people began filing into the room, while Charisse and Delilah were still out of sight as Mother Tibideau told one of the others to make sure there were no uninitiated people in the room. I felt that same feeling all over again—that same feeling I had when I was at the campus church that made me crawl around on the floor. It was not as strong as before because I knew what was happening to me and had the will to fight it along with everyone else. I surprised myself and began to say the things I heard everyone say all day at church and at the dinner table. I started calling on Jesus and pleading the blood, saying "glory glory glory" and "yea yea yea". Anything I heard one of the others say, I said it too. I even got bold and addressed The Blacksmith by name, denouncing his hold on my life, denouncing the coldness, the detachment, the lack of love, lack of compassion, the distrust, everything I could think of that plagued me. At Mother Tibideau's urging, I denounced unforgiveness and asked God to help me forgive my grandmother and mother for what they had done. I prayed for my mother to know Jesus so that we could try to live for God together.

And it was when I confessed that I would forgive that I was thrown to the floor and for a moment felt I was going blind. I felt someone lead me by the hand to the couch and I could smell something spicy as all the women kinfolk began humming and rubbing the spicy ointment all over my head, hands, and feet. I remembered I kept sighing heavily over and over like my body was the earth about to bring something forth. Then it felt like my heart was about to jump out of my chest. As I clutched it, I felt something being ripped from me. My water broke and I began to sing what sounded like a dirge.

We spent the rest of the evening settling the earth beneath my feet that had been trampled by my mother's rage. Minnie Lee and Sally were in and out of sight praying over the house, and going into each room and pleading the blood of Jesus. Charisse was in Mother Tibideau's room taking a power nap. I peeked in and saw that she slept soundly and was not contorted into strange positions or moaning in her sleep like she usually did. For that reason alone I knew we were in a good house. I was sure that Mother Tibideau was darn near virginal, and Charisse needed her bed to put some virtue back into her body by osmosis.

Again I was left alone with no one to talk to as everyone was doing their own thing. At first I began to feel the sting of rejection for no reason, but the feeling of togetherness was so palpable that I made an effort to fight my feelings. Plus, I was afraid Mother Tibideau would pick up on my feelings somehow and appear out of nowhere with a stern look and something to say. Instead of continually looking at my watch to see how long it took someone to notice I was in the living room all by myself, I decided to go out to the porch and take in the night air. To my fortune, Chuck was sitting out there in a rocking chair not doing too much. As I approached him from behind, he turned his head to look up at me. It was then I realized the green in his eyes that were the color of jade and how it matched beautifully with his sandy brown hair that swooped over one eye. He periodically flung his head to the side so that he could see out of his right eye, which was the one that hid behind the swoop. When I came into the room, the swoop moved out of the way on its own. It reminded me of doors opening for the bride to come down the aisle. I could not believe I had such thoughts, but I liked the newness of feeling that part my heart. I was glad I did not share in my mother's hatred of the color holiness white.

"Come on in, Lady of the Hour," Chuck summoned. "I was hoping you'd come out here so we could finish our chat we had earlier."

Not easily flattered, I was. I wanted to finish our conversation too, but figured everyone's thoughts concerning me would revolve around the crazy events. But I was wrong. I was just another person in the house and before I had a chance to determine the subject, Chuck had picked up where we left off.

"I remember I was asking you about your friends."

Fresh out of strong prayers and fighting spirits, I didn't feel it was appropriate to be defensive. "I'm sorry Chuck, but I don't know why we should talk about that," I said, ignoring my inner plea to not be defensive.

"Well, I'm sorry. I hope this doesn't offend you but I was always curious about you."

"But we just met," I said smartly.

"But I didn't just see you."

I became nervous at the thought of Chuck saying I was the exotic black jelly bean in a bag full of colors, or even scarier, that he had a crush on me. I chose to keep my mouth shut and let him continue to tell on himself.

"I mean, I don't know. This might sound crazy to you because you are new in the faith and all, but when I saw you..."

"Hey! Party on the porch?"

The dead had arisen. It was Charisse sucking up all the air again. I could not hide my agitation. I became a maniac in my mind as the butterflies fluttered furiously and tried to escape my stomach through the highway of my esophagus, but I swallowed them back down because butterflies do not return to their vomit by uttering nonsense to people who choose to remain caterpillars. Chuck saw my disdain and gave me a look to let me know that conversation would not be our last. I began to get the feeling that Chuck always picked up where he left off.

Mother Tibideau came to the porch and announced that it was time for us to head back to campus. Thankfully we had an early dinner, which gave us time to mill around and relax without rushing back. The drive was a little over an hour and I was looking forward to being in the same space with Chuck and secretly hoping he'd sit next to me. Michael would stay behind and return in the morning, while Delilah caught a ride with some campus students who wanted to go out for coffee. The rest of us had classes the next day, so we had to . Since we came down on the church bus, we had no way back except to drive. So, Mother Tibideau gave Chuck the keys to the third car and told him to drive carefully. Surely Chuck was not going to drive one of her Cadillacs back to campus, as it was not a car for a young man. Butt lo and behold, the garage door opened and there was an old- school Mustang in the garage looking shiny as a buffalo nickel.

"Mother Tibideau!" Charisse exclaimed. "Let me find out!"

"Oh hush girl! You ain't ready for me," Mother Tibideau quipped.

"Noooooo she ain't!" Minnie Lee chimed in. "She still got it, baby! Sunglasses on, top down, and wig bolted tight to brave the wind!"

Everyone laughed at the thought of Mother Tibideau, patron saint of all things white and holy, driving custom 5-speed, 4-door, cherry red, vintage Mustang whenever she wanted to feel high school fine again.

"I'm from NOLA, baby. That's how we do it! Hey now! Watch yourself!"

Mother Tibideau's sharp wit confirmed all the more that she was kin to me, and if I still wasn't convinced, what she said to Charisse afterward sealed the deal.

"Ah ah ah!" she said to Charisse as she tried to climb into the front seat. "You get in the back!"

My dear great aunt, gave me a wink. I was to ride shotgun with Chuck and daydream about us being a couple. She was not bad for a woman in white after all.

The ride back to campus was surreal as I sat close enough to Chuck to smell the residue of his cologne on his shirt collar. Fahrenheit was all the rage amongst the guys on campus and I loved it. I didn't want to say too much with Charisse in the car because she would interrupt anything good that came out of either of our mouths. For whatever reason, the person that I called one of my best friends became an enemy in one day. It seemed as though the new person I was becoming was antagonistic to the person she was.

"You know back at the house," Charisse began, "Mother Tibideau told me all my business."

I didn't say a word because I knew she would keep talking anyway.

"She told me about my father and sister and how they did stuff to me."

It was the yin and the yang she talked about the night before we left home.

"Charisse, you know you are in a car with a stranger, right?" I said with all the authority and disgust I could muster. As the words left my mouth, I could see Chuck tense up.

"Chuck, I'm…I'm sorry. I didn't mean it like that. I mean…"

"I know what you meant. Hey, we all saw some stuff tonight that was reserved for only a few eyes and ears, so it's no big deal now. What's one more thing?"

"Thank you Chucky!" Charisse said as she wagged her tail like a young puppy. "Anyway, before my *mother* interrupted me, I was saying that Mother Tibideau said she had a vision of my sister holding me down while my father…"

"Charisse!" I screamed. "Nobody wants to hear that! Nobody wants to hear that! Just stop it!"

"Are you the only one who can be heard around here? Are you the only one who can find out about herself from somebody? Stop telling me what to do!"

"Nobody wants to hear that nasty mess!"

"My life is nasty! My daddy is nasty! I'm nasty! It's not my fault my daddy touched me! It's not my fault my sister held me down in my sleep and let my father trap me! It's not my fault my mother died knowing he was a child molester and didn't make no arrangements for somebody to come save me! How would you feel if you felt thrown away all of your life?"

"Charisse, you are not a reject!" I interjected.

"How would you know? How would you know?"

I didn't know what to do with this All of a Sudden Charisse who finally decided to be honest about her feelings without being vague. And she was raging as though each shade of red was fighting to see who was the reddest. That moment was the closest I ever came to her deepest thoughts about the way she lived. There was no more clamming up, faking it through the smile, and getting drunk to numb the pain. Charisse was always kinetic, never verbal. You knew she was in pain because of her attempts at suicide or her treks to my house in the middle of the night. But her hurt was never articulated in song, poem, or conversation. There was no griot to pass down stories about her life in the absence of her own voice. Charisse had finally blown her stack after years of vacillating between being happy go lucky and depressed, but never overt anger. She had a right to be angry and I finally felt it. And I also knew that I spent our entire friendship protecting her, but the one person I could never protect her from was herself.

The whole time Chuck had been silent and allowed my longtime friend to lose herself in dark conversation because he probably felt it needed to happen. I only remember him mumbling something as he rubbed his chin in confusion. He said, "It jumped on her." I did not know what he meant but thought maybe he knew better than to get in between two black women he barely knew, Jesus or no Jesus.

"You don't understand how I've been feeling all these years laughing to keep from crying, being the butt of everyone's jokes!" Charisse continued. "You don't know how it feels to have your virginity taken away before you reach the age of 10 and have your mother so drunk that she would leave the house when she knew your father was going to do something. Let me say what I want to say! You know how it feels to always be sore from my father poking me at night with all kinds of stuff? I grew up before I was supposed to! My cat is raggedy and I'm ashamed to let anybody see it! You think I always want to have sex in the dark?"

Charisse's unfiltered diatribe caused me to slip into a barrage of hand gestures and hard "Long Islandese" with an "Oh my god, are you serious?" to "Are you kidding me right now with that?" and one or two, "Get outta here already!" followed by a, "She's crazy that girl!" and ending with a "This moron" that took me down a few octaves and slid between my jaws, which was resurrected by "Charisse you're killing me here!"

"Killing you? Killing you? I'm the one who's dying! I might be HIV positive. And another thing…I'm pregnant! What you got to say about that, Dice?"

I swallowed my gum before the flavor had a chance to make a run for it. I hated losing my gum while it was still juicy, but it was inevitable. Charisse revealed that she may be carrying her father's child because she had gone home the weekend before she was with Vince and her father molested her. I could not understand how, as a woman who was finally old enough to drink, drive, vote, and say "No" to a man's advances, that her father was still able to lay with her. It was not like she was a child who was forced or afraid. It reminded me of my mother and Reesie's assessment of Charisse one night after her many runs to my house for refuge.

"She likes it," my mother offered while watching Reesie pour a glass of wine. "Got to. Why you think she cling to that man like he's a long lost lover? She come running over here after every episode, seem like. Then she runs back."

"She got that syndrome," Reesie concluded. "What you call it? Stockings Syndrome."

"Not Stockings, you wheat colored chaff! Oh my god, I bet every fleur de lis wilts at the sound of your ignorant voice. It's Stockbridge Syndrome."

"Stockholm!" I yelled downstairs.

"I think somebody is supposed to be asleep and not in grown folks' conversation! And don't you fix your mouth to answer me back and say goodnight, I'm sorry, or I've fallen and can't get up because I'm assuming you are asleep right now. Am I correct?"

I feigned a light snore and it grew louder and louder and louder until I realized the snore in my memory was the growl of Charisse's voice.

"I'm pregnant with my child and my sibling! I can't raise a child! I can't suffer and die! All this praying and touching foreheads and stuff and God didn't do nothing for me! Even God don't want me!"

While I gasped at the thought of a pregnancy, Chuck interjected with "Jesus loves you!", but it was not enough to stop all of the cylinders that were firing that night.

"If he loved me he would have given me a chance. I never had a chance. I never had a chance to own myself and feel like somebody. I hate my life. I hate my life and I don't care how many people tell me it will get better because it never does. I hate the sound of the rise and fall of my chest because it means I have another minute on earth. I'm tired, Suzi. I'm tired and I keep repeating myself, and my bad luck keeps repeating itself, and nobody ever takes their finger off my pulse. As long as I'm still breathing I'm a specimen to somebody. I'm tired for real this time."

I screamed at Charisse until I could not scream anymore because I did not want her to play the victim. I did not want her to steal the show hollering about stuff she should have been used to going through, and by that point be able to avoid. She had to be tough, suck it up, and deal with the choices she made even after being able to get away from her father for good. She chose to keep going back home whenever he said he missed her. She chose to sleep with him even though she could have either stayed with my mother or stayed in North Carolina. Charisse was a self-sabotager and always wanted someone to feel sorry for her.

There were so many people in her situation that wished they had a friend like me to be there for her, or a mother like mine who, despite not being too keen on anyone that did not bear her last name, still welcomed Charisse into our home and treated her like family. I felt Charisse should have been grateful that things were not worse. But then I entertained the thought that maybe, just maybe, Charisse *was* in the worst part of life. Just maybe there was no one worse off than her and that she truly *was* the bottom. Then what? Then I would be embarrassed over my insensitivity and for pretending to know about something I never went through, and for preaching a sermon—extemporaneously at that—with no frame of reference, scripture, or even endorsement from God, but just my own self-righteous thoughts because I believed I was too strong to be as much of a screw up as she was. I had a mother who, in her own unorthodox way, blanketed me with all the physical protection anyone could muster. I did not know what it was like to be wide open and preyed upon all of my life. I wondered what would be the price for me sitting high and looking low. It was then I realized my compassion for Charisse was not in the form she needed most. While me protecting her and making her feel like family was a good show of friendship, what she needed most was to be understood.

As my thoughts taught me more than any textbook could, I was interrupted by a nightmare that was in the making all night long. I soon came to regret that we were in a four door car as the back driver's side door flung open, headlights flashed, Chuck slammed on the brakes, and I saw Charisse in the rear view mirror rolling down the highway into oncoming traffic. The butterflies I had on reserve for my time with Chuck came raging out of my stomach and through my mouth, each one turning back and hovering at eye level to stare me down. The degree of contempt those butterflies exuded was greater than that of a rose called by another name. It was still a rose, but it was mad as hell and more scarlet than the "A" on Hester Prynne's chest. They flew over to Charisse as she lay lifeless in the road. The car that hit her as she dove out of Mother Tibideau's car had crashed into a tree and another vehicle, in an attempt to swerve away from both the crashed car and Charisse, had rolled into a ditch. All of the life in my body left me as my best friend slept in a pool of her own crimson blood all because I did not want to hear her truth. I realized that my inability to be compassionate made me a murderer and I wondered how many people were killed daily because no one wanted to hear their problems.

I ran over to Charisse and was afraid to touch her before I moved a bone out of place, and said I'm sorry over and over again. I told her she could come to my house and my mother would cook something for us to eat. I reminded her that she could sleep in my room instead of the room with the dolls so that we could sit up and talk and she could finish telling me how she felt. Then we'd get up the next day and call Creepy and we all would go to the park and sit on the bleachers and talk about nothing while overlooking an empty baseball field where people hit homeruns of a different kind. We would look to our right and see people on the basketball courts with their t-shirts off or tied around their waists as they played for bragging rights. Or we could watch the kids on the swings who disappeared behind the hedges that lined the fence, then they would reappear at a 45 degree angle wit squeals of elevated delight. I wanted to turn back the clock so bad that I hated time, that ancient thief who stole every second, every minute, every hour, and everybody.

As I knelt beside Charisse, Chuck was on the other side of her praying in tongues, lightly touching her forehead, and commanding that every bone be put back into place and that her spirit would return to her body. He rebuked the spirit of witchcraft, anger, and murder, and told the spirit that had followed Charisse and me on our drive to school freshman year that it would not accomplish its mission and had to return to sender. And that meant it would go back to my house, to my mother, and kill her. And that could mean I would have two funerals to attend.

As I watched time eke out a dishonest wage in the hospital waiting room, I buried my face in Chuck's chest as I tried to make sense of God trying to make me choose. If we prayed for Charisse and she lived, my mother would die. If we prayed for my mother to be protected from her own deeds, Charisse would die. And if I continued in mass confusion at being overwhelmed by my life becoming a movie, *I* would die. As my thoughts ran carefree, they were interrupted by a sure fact that I had forgotten about.

"Chuck, what did you mean when you said something jumped on Charisse?"

Chuck seemed reluctant to explain as he probably did not mean to let it slip. But knowing I would not let it go, he obliged me. He mentioned that when someone experienced being set free from a plaguing condition, sometimes the spirit responsible for the bondage would come out of that person but enter someone else who was not under God's protection. Mother Tibideau said she wanted the uninitiated out of the room, but when Charisse and Delilah were done in the room, Charisse was nosing around and Chuck was too busy praying to break his stride and get her out of sight. Him not doing so probably caused Charisse to be infected with what was on me, as her outburst in the car was out of character. Her actions were identical to my thoughts; loud, confusing, and angry. Because I was an introvert and Charisse was an extrovert, in Charisse The Blacksmith put voice and action to the thoughts that were in my head. He said he would return, but I did not know it would be for my friend. If she died it would be my fault.

We were in the hospital for what seemed like hours as we awaited word on Charisse's prognosis. My brother, Michael, was on his way with Mother Tibideau and the Holiness Twins in tow. The whole time we were in the waiting room, Chuck held me in his arms while ignoring the funny look or two we received from the long time residents of the small town. After I had bitten off my last nail, the doctor came out to us and was completely silent. He looked at us as though he was apologizing for not having power over life and death. My mind knew what he was about to say, but my heart spoke before he had a chance. Soon my hands and feet began to compete with my heart for who could be the best mourner, and my tears ran up and down the hallway trying to avoid any attempt at wiping them up with leftover McDonald's napkins. I could see them running in circles and bumping into each other while my eyes tried to stare them back into submission. But it did not work. Chuck had to summon the strength of ten men to hold me back from hurting myself. It could not be true. Charisse could not be dead.

"She lost too much blood and her injuries are too serious," the doctor began. "We did all we could."

"But God has the last word!" It was Mother Tibideau who had her Bible in one hand and a bottle of oil in the other. "Take me to her."

"M'am," the doctor said.

"It's Minister M'am to you! Take me to her before I lump you in with the demons I'm about to cast out!"

Mother Tibideau was furious at the thought of someone standing between her and the power she had in each hand. The doctor saw that it was no use stopping God's Champion. She marched into Charisse's room like Miss Sophia marched through the cornfields to tell Celie to mind her business. A storm was coming.

"Charisse!" Mother Tibideau commanded. "I command your spirit to return to your body in the name of Jesus! It is not your time!"

I continued to scream, asking Chuck what was Mother Tibideau doing and how could anyone come back alive after they were dead. Mother Tibideau seemed used to commotion as she ignored my various queries about the validity of her science and continued to hover over Charisse like a mother eagle guarding her hatchlings. While she continued to command, and demand, and rebuke, and bind, and rebuke again, Charisse turned to look at me. No one else seemed to notice as, to them, her eyes were slammed shut. But I saw them wide open and staring at me. I opened my mouth to scream and Charisse raised a cold finger to her mouth to tell me to remain silent.

"Suzi," Charisse's spirit called out to me. "There is a legion around me."

"A what?" I asked silently

"A legion for they are many. They are mad at you."

"What are you talking about?"

"You got saved. They said you had an army of angels around you. Chuck too. That's why they couldn't crash the car. They got in my head and threw me out of the car because I had no angels."

"What?"

"Tell Mother Tibideau to stop praying for me. I don't want to live. I think I am going towards the light. But she needs to keep praying for you. They are going to come after you. They really want you."

"Charisse, you can't go! You can't go!"

"Suzi, I'm tired of life. Let me go towards the light. I'm trying to go but Mother Tibideau got the inside line with God or something. It's weird. I see a whole bunch of stuff in this room. You got a big angel standing over you. He is huge! Oh my God, he is so big. He looks mean like if anyone touches you, y'all got beef. And Chuck has two standing next to him. They look like twins. Michael got a few, I think because he is a preacher. One of them is fighting something—I can't see it. And Mother Tibideau...the one she got is taller than the ceiling and it's bright, so I don't know if it is even an angel. This room is full of stuff."

Thinking I was going crazy as I sunk deeper into indescribable grief, I shut my eyes tight to see if I opened them again, Charisse would be to me as she was to the others. Dead. When I returned to the visual world, she was still staring at me with soulless eyes.

"Why don't you just come back?" I begged. "What is so bad about life?"

"I told you in the car. You didn't listen to me. I guess the devil showed you better than he could tell you. I guess when people cry out for help and no one listens, the devil comes in and lends an ear. Oooh, I sounded like Mother Tibideau just now!"

I marveled at how she could joke from the dead.

"He got strong hands too," Charisse's corpse continued. "Strong enough to move my hand against my will and open the car door. I would never go out like that. Matter of fact, let me tell you how it felt before something happens and you try it too."

"And why would I kill myself?"

"Because no one understands you."

"Why do I need to people to understand me?"

"So that you can feel like you matter to somebody."

I ignored her post-mortem pronouncement about me and recognized it as a projection of her feelings about herself. Charisse was always an object and never a person except to my mother, sometimes Reesie, and me. And at times my mother had one too many "tsk tsk" thoughts and words about Charisse, but nevertheless she was still human when she entered our home. When I thought about it, Charisse made me feel human too. I thought I did more for her than she did for me, but I realized what she did for me could not be seen but could only be felt. She loved me like a sister, never judged me, never asked me to be more than what I was, and challenged me to offer the same. While I went to great lengths to protect Charisse from physical hurt and offered a safe haven, I was not sure if I offered the emotional buffer she truly needed. Despite that, she never charged me for it until it was time for her to die.

When I got past the gravity of Charisse's words, my body remembered to wince at the thought of her describing what it was like to throw herself from a car and feel the sting of fresh tires rolling over her body. True to her tacky ways, she felt compelled to tell me. She offered what it felt like to lose control of her senses, which she described as an outer body experience where all you see is red and tiny lights flickering all over the place, kind of like when you look at the sun and keep blinking. I was all too familiar with that. Then she said her head felt light like a feather and there was a buzzing sound in her ears that caused her to not hear herself as she spoke. I knew about that, too. Before she knew it, her voice had gotten so high that her words were indecipherable and all of her senses collided with one another. My own antics were returning to me through my friend as she had yet to say something I was unaware of. And at the point when things were the most coded and the most confusing was when she felt compelled to stop the madness and throw herself out of the car.

Charisse said it felt like a movie at first because everything happened so quickly. She remembered seeing the pine trees and noticing how close her face was to the yellow line in the highway. Charisse said her last thought was, "I'm free from him!" before she smelled hot rubber and gasoline. She felt her ribs buckle under the weight of the car's driver's side tire. She said it sounded like wood against wood shuffling in her chest, and she felt a massive splinter pierce her skin. That was when the blood began to spill out of her mouth and she heard me screaming, more tires screeching, and someone laughing in the background that sounded like an evil grin in a woman's voice. She said it was much like one of the voices she heard in the basement at my graduation party.

Charisse probably wanted to take the liberty to say the voice belonged to my mother since she was dead and safe from a whooping. With her luck, Mother Tibideau would be successful in raising her from the dead and my mother would then be able to make good on that whooping. But my mother loved Charisse and would never hurt her; it was the demons she thought worked for her. In the short time I got to know more about God, I realized two things: the devil was self-employed and answers to no one—not even people who do evil. By the time I had snapped back into reality and questioned if I really did have a conversation with Charisse's spirit, the last words I heard Mother Tibideau say were, "Return to sender!"

"Sister no!" Minnie Lee cried out. "Not another one! No, sister, no!"

The two sisters begged their older, more powerful sister to back off returning the spirit to its owner and I knew from earlier that day it had to be my mother. But, I did not know why Minnie Lee felt the need to protest so profusely. If all that happened was evil, why would she interfere with the remedy? And was my mother really going to die? Who was the other one Minnie Lee spoke of?

"Esther!" Mother Tibideau commanded. "It's either you or the girl. Take it back in Jesus' name."

As Mother Tibideau continued to rant and rave in Jesus' name, the room grew cold and I could smell sulfur coming from Charisse's direction. Mother Tibideau signaled her sisters to lie across Charisse's body and fight for her soul. I could not bear to tell them that Charisse did not want to fight; she wanted to die. I could not tell them that I felt like I was losing my mind in the hospital room because dead people don't talk, yet I had a conversation my mind really didn't think I had.

Throughout the ordeal Pastor Michael sat quietly in the corner looking as though he wanted to pray but could not. His face was frozen like he felt the battle was above his pay grade. It was either that or he felt an affinity for the woman he never got to know except by way of witchcraft and doing battle to free his only sister.

"Chuck," my great aunt called out, "get Suzi out of here now! Michael, you too."

"But..." Michael started.

"I said out! This battle is personal. It's for those of us of the Apostolic order. The old time holiness church! Out!"

As we exited the room, I looked back and saw another vision. This time it was not Charisse telling me how tired she was or what death visions she had in the room. Instead, I saw little demons popping out of Charisse's body attempting to push Minnie Lee and Sally either off of her or off of them. All of the demons looked like sex organs, blood, unborn fetuses, and crossed eyes as Mother Tibideau aimed to rid Charisse of not only the demons that tried to come after me, but the one's that always plagued her. I did not know how I could see those things and not lose my mind right there on the spot.

After what seemed like an eternity, the room fell so silent that you could hear hair shedding onto the floor. The door opened—or so it seemed—and two men walked out of the room. The first was a bright angel with a long robe in an array of colors. He carried Charisse in his arms and walked towards me. He looked me in the eye while Charisse's lifeless body was draped over his God-sized hands. He then lifted her up into the air, looked up to what I assumed was heaven, and asked, "Do you accept?" Then the ceiling opened and a bright ray of light took Charisse from the angel and lifted her body—her *spirit*—up, up, and up until I could see her no more.

The second being was tall man about 8 feet tall with a black hooded robe, a round wrinkled face the color of a paper bag, and eyes that were white as chalk. He walked out of the room with a sword hanging by his side with blood on its tip. I noticed one of his arms was limp as though it was paralyzed, and his mouth was twisted to one side. At that moment my pager went off. It was Reesie.

"Oh God!" I screamed into the phone when I called returned Reesie's page. I became weak and fell into Chuck's arms. Reesie told me my mother had to be rushed to the hospital. She said my mother had gotten a warning from Federline that something was going to happen and that she needed to call a meeting in the basement. Federline, Rita, and a few other people who frequented my mother's basement parties were down below chanting and screaming and twirling while downing bottles of Jamaican white rum. Reesie heard Federline scream that "they" were coming for her and that the spirits she sent out were charging back to her like bulls rushing a lone matador. They were all confused as they thought the spirits worked for them and did their bidding, yet soon realized the devil professed to have no master. Reesie remembered hearing a commotion upstairs and when she reached the top, all of my mother's dolls had fallen off the shelf and were turned face down like they were bowing before a being greater than themselves.

"Baby Suzi, I think your mother had a stroke," Reesie revealed. "Federline carried her out of the basement and her arms were dangling and all limp. Her mouth was twisted all the way to the other side of her face. I don't know what happened, but I think your mother got in too deep this time. Too deep! It's going down the same way it went down with Mama. I can't believe this is happening to us again!"

I was so overwhelmed to the point where I could not cry or scream. I threw myself over Charisse's body while the others retreated and realized God had the last word, and her best friend should have the last cry. Everyone seemed to be at peace knowing that Charisse had her final deliverance and was ready to go home and be with God. She did not know him in the way Christians say a person should know God, but who knows the conversation she had with him while alive and resting in Mother

Tibideau's blessed room? In no way, shape or form could I say she was a candidate for Hell after having been a victim all of her life. No way. But my mother was a different story and I felt she would possibly suffer the same fate as my grandmother. The circumstances of my grandmother's death, which were never told to me, must have come by way of my great aunt who was not afraid to do battle with the dark. I was only told my grandmother died on her knees with her eyes looking up at the ceiling. I realized at that moment why my mother hated the women in pure white so much. In her eyes they and the Christian God were murderers.

As I lay on the hospital floor with Chuck holding me in his arms, I began a battle within myself. Somehow I felt it was my fault that my mother and Charisse suffered the consequences of me saying yes to a God who was supposed to be merciful. I thought Jesus was the only one who could suffer for the sins of another. I gained a new family only to lose the one I had to a God who was supposed to add and not subtract. The thought gave me no closure.

I learned that Mother Tibideau and crew would make a trip to New York to see Augustine's daughter who laid in a hospital bed knotted like an old tree. Michael had convinced his adopted mother that he wanted to lay eyes on his birth mother and let her see the blessing that came from her womb. Everyone thought it best that I didn't return home but rather stay and focus on school. It was as if they knew she would make it out of the ordeal, but how would I reconcile the fact that the people my mother hated told me to stay away from her? I could not live with myself and decided to make the trip despite Mother Tibideau's protests. I made arrangements with my professors to submit my work upon my return and took the first plane smoking out of North Carolina. I declined to drive up with Mother Tibideau and crew because I wanted to beat them there. I wanted to survey what was happening in the house before all hell broke loose with the long lost family showing up.

The news of Charisse's death spread on the campus like wildfire, but strangely no one seemed to be shocked or saddened. It became even more real to me how inhuman Charisse must have felt. Delilah, who had missed all of the action, opted to pack Charisse's belongings and correspond with her family to help with arrangements. She even offered to buy her a nice, white dress to be buried in when I told her that her siblings probably picked over her belongings that were left behind at home. Delilah wanted Charisse to be buried in the color of the virtue that was taken from her by her father, and even mentioned that she could somewhat relate to Charisse's sexual abuse, although she never outright used the word "molested".

"Delilah, I want to thank you for being there for my friend. I don't know anyone who would care enough to do this."

"Suzi, this is how we do things," Delilah explained. "At one time in my life I wouldn't care about helping anyone but myself, but God gave me a heart to be there for people and now I can't help it. I feel compelled to give of myself. It's no problem. I didn't really know Charisse, but I could feel her pain. It's the least I could do. I know what it's like to have my body intruded upon."

"What do you mean intruded upon? You mean *that*?"

"No, but it could have been had I not been so skinny."

"Are you kidding me? What does size have to do with a pervert being a pervert?"

"Even perverts have their own special brand of taste. I got away because I was an ugly duckling. That was when I began to protect myself because I felt if that person would do something like that to me, anyone would."

I was surprised at Delilah's admission as before Charisse's passing, she would never delve into any details of her life other than she was saved, truly saved, and fully saved. But saved from what? She never told. And maybe that was the plastic I saw in her smile because behind the straight, pearly white teeth was a story of stains, cavities, and chipped enamel. We talked long into the night partly because I needed to listen to someone in honor of Charisse, and I supposed Delilah was confronted with what could have happened to her had she not met God.

"Suzi, you would not believe me, but I was mad all of the time. I was a ticking time bomb ready to explode. God had to save me radically or not at all. That's why your harshness towards me never made me blink. Dealing with you was really me dealing with the old me."

Delilah continued to explain how when she met God, she had no religion just like me. She lived in a household where bad luck and the devil were more of a topic of conversation than an omnipotent and benevolent God. It wasn't until she felt completely alone that she realized she needed something bigger than herself to give her life meaning and teach her how to love. She got on her knees and asked God to reveal himself to her. That's when someone approached her, and as she did me, and invited her to Bible study. The topic was "Who Is God?" and that sealed the deal for her.

Even though Delilah was happy in her newfound faith, her family had mixed emotions once it seemed she was serious about it. They were okay with her when she went to church once a week and lived her life as usual. But when she began going a few times a week, then coming home and praying and confessing the things she believed God to do for her, everyone thought she lost her mind. She even heard she was in a cult from one of her old high school teachers. She felt so alienated from her own family that she adopted the church as her family, and she did whatever she could to increase the distance between flesh and blood. For her, alienation had a softer touch than being misunderstood. She even lost a few friends because they felt she was too strict, yet when she loosened up as they had suggested, those same friends called her a hypocrite.

"Suzi, I was really hurting. The day I gave my life to Christ, in my family's eyes I lost the right to be a human being, to be imperfect, to not get it right sometimes. I even had one relative tell me to give up my faith because as far as she was concerned, I was not a real Christian."

"Why? Didn't she know all you went through?"

"She did, but when you confront people with the truth about themselves, they lash out and hit below the belt. I let her have that because if she really knew what God did for me, if she knew that it wasn't until I became a Christian that I was able to look her in the eye and love her rather than hate her, she'd regret her words. I know what God did in my heart and if it were not for him, I'd either be dead or off on an island by myself. I understand that those types of attacks come with the territory. To people who don't understand this faith, you will never be a good enough Christian. I accept that."

I was both intrigued and overwhelmed by Delilah's impromptu confession that I began to cry. I cried for her, I cried for Charisse, and I cried for myself. I did not have concerns about being misunderstood or ostracized or any of the things that came with changing paradigms. What I cried for was the knowledge that I would have to go into the inner sanctum of my being, and disturb the sleeping giants that had lived in my soul for so long and made me a prisoner in my mind. I would have to open up and learn what it was like to be vulnerable, to trust, and to learn how to have a family who was normal and loved me before they even met me. I wasn't even sure if I deserved it, but Mother Tibideau had a way of finalizing what one should feel about anything. If she said it, so shall it be.

In addition to Delilah's show of genuine concern, Mari had heard of Charisse's death and offered her condolences via telephone. She also mentioned she learned of my mother's stroke and that it was rumored her condition was due to God's vengeance. Mari briefly chatted to make sure I was okay, but by choice I remained unaffected. I did not want to mistake the moment for a rekindling our friendship, nor did I want to open myself up to be hurt again. Knowing Mari was decent enough to care was good enough for me. I did not have the strength to be manipulated by the idea of needing her or her family's approval of me any longer, and I resolved to let them go. I thought I may as well deal with the pain of losing everyone at once so that I could heal all at once and move on with my life.

"I'm sorry I didn't hang in there with you. I'm so sorry," was the last thing I heard Mari say as we spoke for the last time. Ironically, those were the same words I should have said to Charisse.

After I packed my things to fly out the next morning and felt satisfied enough to finally go to bed, I got a phone call wishing me a good night's sleep and to be ready in the morning. Chuck's swooping voice was just what I needed to tuck me in.

"I will make sure you get to the airport on time. We can do breakfast if you want. You shouldn't fly on an empty stomach," Chuck advised.

"Breakfast would be good," I replied. "Even on a short flight I hate being hungry."

"I know this is a dumb observation given the circumstances, but were you just crying?"

I gave a reluctant yes and briefly recapped the topic of conversation with Delilah and Mari. I was surprised at my openness. I didn't even care to ask why as I began to learn that Chuck never spoke an idle word.

"Okay," he continued. "I want to say I'm glad that you are continuing to let yourself be present with your feelings. I'm not trying to psychoanalyze you, though."

"Feels like it," I said in a half-joking manner.

"I know. I'm just little protective, you know. I'll try not to psychobabble too much around you. And speaking of protection, I will honor your body's need to rest so I will say goodnight. I love..."

"What?" I interrupted with the speed of Hermes.

"I was about to say I love sleep myself. But since you thought I was going to say something else, I will say that I believe in love at first sight. Well, in your case, a few sights."

Even though Chuck tried to get me off the phone for my sake, I did not want the conversation to end. He had me curious, intrigued, and all of the above, and I decided that I would have to wrestle with sleep before I let the conversation go.

"Chuck, let me ask you something."

"Shoot."

"How...I mean, you know. How, um, alright...you know I'm black, right?"

"So?"

"I just wanted to know if you noticed."

"I notice it just as much as Jesus does."

"Chuck, I'm serious. I mean, you got swagger for a white boy and all but..."

"For the record, my great grandmother was black and Chickasaw Indian."

"I knew it!"

"So is it okay? Can we continue getting to know each other? I mean, are you okay with a little cream in your coffee?"

"Oh you are more than cream. You are milk. Whole milk! At least in winter."

We both shared a laugh that warmed my heart in all the places it needed. I imagined myself stirring whole milk in my coffee in winter, and how I would curl up with my feet underneath me and giggle at every word that came out of Chuck's mouth. I felt softer than the feathers in his great-grandmother's regalia. After spending an additional hour on the phone, Chuck put his foot down and said it was time to say good night. He reminded me that we had breakfast the next morning and he did not want to rush our meal.

And the evening and the morning were the second day as I finally arrived at the airport after a breakfast that was a continuation of our discussion about milk, coffee, and feathers. Being the gentleman that he already showed himself to be, Chuck gave me a stern look to remind me that he was to open the door for me and carry my bags because that's how Tennessee men do things. Out of respect for me, Chuck did not do what some men usually did and attempt to kiss me, as he felt it was best that we continued to get to know each other. With all of the consoling that was going on at Mother Tibideau's house and at the hospital, we had touched enough. He did not want to mistake those moments for opportunities to do other things, so he opted to take the holy route and get to know me by talking and not touching. If I did not admit I was slightly disappointed I'd be fooling myself, but at the same time I respected a man who seemed to be everything my mother said a man could not be. I was beginning to like the Jesus life more and more.

I finally arrived at the airport thinking Reesie would be there waiting for me. Instead it was Creepy who was sent to do the honors. He said my aunt was too distraught to drive. She was at odds with her feelings about my conversion and connection to the banned members of the family, thinking that I may have been brainwashed to conspire with them against my mother. Knowing that I would be stepping into an awkward climate coming into contact with Reesie, I queried Creepy about all that happened.

"Your mother was in the house by herself at first talking on the phone with Federline, telling him something was happening in the house and she needed him to come over and help her."

"Tell me exactly what happened, like visuals and everything," I asked, reveling in my ability to understand that world a little more than before.

"That's funny," Creepy marveled. "You were never interested in details before."

Creepy shook off his marvel and shared how my mother was in the kitchen washing dishes when she looked over her shoulder and saw one of the dolls from the room where Charisse always slept, lying on the floor face down. Since she was the only one in the house, Reesie knew there was only one way it could have gotten downstairs. She then heard lamentation coming from the room, ran up the stairs to see what the commotion was, and saw an angel with a flaming sword forbidding her to go any further.

"That was when she called Federline because she realized she was fighting with God. He told her to call everyone over. It wasn't long after everybody got there that your mother was twisted into a knot."

While I felt sorry for my mother, I learned that if you played by the devil's rules, you'll reap the devil's reward. I began to question my own self because I could not understand how I became a Christian and my mother became my enemy. Had I no feelings?

"Don't fight with yourself," Creepy advised, sensing that I was in some turmoil. "You did a good thing becoming a Christian. I always saw there was hope for you. For me? Not so much."

"Creepy, what are you talking about?"

"You know what I'm talking about. You think I could come by your house and not be afraid for no reason? I know all about what your mother does. I come from a long line of voodoo. Long line. They tried to get me, too. The man in the black robe came to me as a child and asked me if I would sell my soul to the devil."

"Did you?"

"I didn't sell my soul, but I made a deal. I got some power, but around you they don't work. Somebody always praying for you. It's like they pray for your protection, and to have a clean heart and mind. I even heard it one day. A lady's voice. She was praying to God the same prayer over and over."

Creepy recited the prayer and I knew instantly who it was. He said the voice would pray for my protection from the crown of my head to the soles of my feet. He said the voice asked for God to protect my comings and goings and to place a hedge of protection around me. Mother Tibideau.

"Man, I been waiting for years for that lady to stop praying so that I could get at you. I finally gave up. You gonna be a virgin all your life, girl."

We both let out a loud laugh as we both knew prayers or no, no man would lay a finger on Esther's child's goodies. After the laugh, Creepy gave me a look and my gaze in return replied that, even at that moment, no such luck.

"Man! Can't get no play? So not even The Man get with you?"

"What "The Man"? And why do you talk like that anyway, like you just came to this country?"

"Why your people *been* in this country and they 'be like' and 'you know what I'm sayin' and 'honey children' and…"

"Honey *chile*!"

"… 'homegirl' this and that and calling each other niggas and fools and stuff. Your mother love that nigga word, man. You don't see no Haitian people calling each other that stuff."

"The Americanized ones do!"

"Right! So my point has been made, my baby."

I knew better than to answer Creepy back on anything he said and simply reminded him to remember we were just friends.

"Yah yah, we know this. So anyway…The Man. You got a man. Every time I light my candle and tell it to bring my bride to me, it blows out. You got a man. And I know he don't look like me because before the fire blows out it gets white hot. Not red, not orange, not yellow—not even a greasy blue flame for spontaneous combustion, but *white* hot. You sleeping with the enemy or what?"

"Creepy."

"You."

Our conversation continued with me dodging any talk of Chuck and focusing on what to expect from my mother's dog pound of cohorts who ran in and out of the house. Creepy suggested that I stay with someone and not in the house by myself. He said the house was angry and I was not mature enough to handle that type of darkness. Even though I was raised in it, I was returning with a new spirit that was antagonistic to the status quo in the house. I went through my mental Rolodex to see who I could stay with. I definitely could not stay at Charisse's house, I was not really talking to Mari, Marie-Colette's people may or may not let me stay based on what they may have heard, and there was definitely no way I could stay at Roger's house since my mother put a demon in him. As I was in the middle of my thoughts, my pager went off. It was Mother Tibideau. Creepy pulled over so that I could use a pay phone.

"Suzi, are you in NY yet?"

"Yes, I am on my way to the house."

"I failed to address your arrangements. You can't go back to your house, so you will stay with us. There will be someone to let you in before we get there."

"Okay. My friend just told me the same thing so I will definitely do that. What is the address?"

When Mother Tibideau gave me the address, my jaw nearly dropped. Same county, same city, and even the same block! Mother Tibideau owned the house across the street from me! My neighbors were people from Mother Tibideau's old church in New York, and once she found that my mother had purchased in that city, she prayed for God to bless her with property there so that she could have someone keep an eye on me and let her know of my comings and goings. She bought the house for her trustworthy friends and they repaid her with their vigilance in keeping watch over me. When I told Creepy, he erupted into laughter so hard that he swerved into another lane.

"I knew it!" he said. "This lady is shrewd! I like her already. She got your life and your cookies sewn up. Man, see if she got a bank account in your name, too. She probably work for the CIA or something. That lady good!"

Creepy went on to say that he knew something was strange about that house, but I didn't know if that was really the case or if he drummed up false memories after learning about its circumstances. He went on to say that he would pass by the house and see something staring out of the window at the thing that was staring out of my window. The thing in my house was dark and the thing in the house across the street was light. He said it was an angel and a demon having a showdown to see who could watch the block the best. But in all of that, I wondered why my mother never said anything about the house as she always swore she had eyes everywhere.

"One thing I know about your God is he knows how to keep secrets. There are some Christians so powerful that no voodoo can work on them."

"Well, Mother Tibideau said no power is greater than God's power, so it won't work on *any* Christian."

"There are different kinds of Christians, girl. Not all of them are powerful. They just tell you that to make themselves look good. That's in First Corinthians. And yea I read the Bible. All Christians are not alike. For a lot of them it is just talk so they can say they belong, but the real stuff happens when they go home. I did tricks on some of them before. My weakest stuff works on the ones that are in church every day, rolling on the floor and speaking in tongues."

"How?"

"All praise and no practice, girl. Your God is powerful but your religion is not. Trust me. I can talk all day about what you people are doing wrong, but I don't want to sidetrack you because you are new."

Even though I was too new to hear most of what Creepy would say, I begged him to tell me anyway. I wanted to know the pitfalls I would encounter that would take me back to the nether lands in my mind. He agreed to tell me a few things, the first being something I was already told. He talked about Christians who had a false sense of themselves, which were the ones who thought going to church all the time and dancing in the aisles made them superior. He brought to my attention again First Corinthians in the Bible where Paul addressed Christians who thought they were better than others because they had spiritual gifts. Those were some of the easiest to deceive because they rested on their works and not God. Then he talked about the ones who were told they had a calling on their lives and were given direct access to the pastor. He said they were easiest to target because they think that in order for them to have gotten that far, God must have special favor on them. They become hungry for acknowledgment and would do anything to keep it, which took them away from the fundamental things they needed to do to maintain their spirituality. They turn their callings into idols and forget about the God of the calling.

"Witches love messing with them," Creepy continued, "because those kinds of Christians are blinded. They see every bad incident as a test or an attack from the devil, so they never get the real problem solved."

The real problem, he claimed, was within *them*. The church was full of people with a victim mentality looking for validation. Those people never admit their faults because they live life with the understanding that all the bad that happened to them was God's plan, and thus do not take responsibility for their contribution to their own suffering. They are taught that people who come against them are jealous or being used by the devil, and the ones who are no longer in their lives were relieved of their friendship duty by God. He said all of that bred false suspicion and paranoia disguised as discernment, and a host of other things that did not unify but rather divided. Christians were to be brothers and sisters, but instead they were subliminally trained to view anyone who did not go along to get along as an enemy or a heretic. He said the best way to divide a church was to pit one person embracing a lie against someone who is not afraid to tell the truth.

"Anybody who introduces change, even if it is needed, is automatically labeled an enemy. All you have to do is get the attention of the person who fights to keep the status quo in the church. You get that person to put their eye on you, your reputation gone! And if that person is close to the pastor and he trusts them, double gone! You could be the answer to somebody's prayer in that place, but for a lot of Christians *different* means *devil*. I just laugh. I could tell you more, but I don't want to…how do you say it…incur the wrath of your God for leading you astray."

"Creepy, I don't know how to take all of this coming from someone who told me they made a deal with the devil."

"Trust me, the devil knows more about God than the ones down here saying they see him and hear his voice. A lot of that stuff that go on in church is fake Christianity with the Bible as a prop. You stick with me and I will teach you how to be a good Christian. Yeah, take me to church one day when you come back to stay. I will show you who is a devil and who is for real."

"But you work for the devil!"

"I'm a snitch, though."

I wanted to ignore that piece of news, but then I remembered through all the talk about voodoo and my love life and secret addresses and fake Christianity, I was not yet bold enough in my faith to tell Creepy that he needed to break his deal with the devil. He knew way more than I did, and while he could be dead wrong in a lot of things, I did not have the spiritual vocabulary to dispute him. It was best for me to just educate myself on how people saw my newfound faith so that I'd have something practical to add to my spiritual knowledge. Embracing Christianity with no religious background left me with no ties to Christian superstition or false doctrine in disguise, so my embrace was strictly for God and God alone.

I was glad when we finally arrived to the house that things looked exactly the way they did when I first left home. True to my mother's stubborn nature, she still had the statues lined up neatly on the lawn. Although I had no plans to stay in the house, I still wanted to go in and check on the place to see how Reesie was doing. Creepy asked if I wanted him to go in with me, as he was not sure how the spirits in the house would receive me since I was under new management. Before I had a chance to respond, Reesie appeared at the door, her eyes pink with new grief.

"Is this your doing?! Is this your doing?!" Reesie screamed between tears. "She was fine until you started with them people!"

Creepy took me by the arm and led me past her as he probably knew she had a speech prepared for me. Reesie turned and looked in disbelief at the blatant lack of acknowledgment from either of us. I knew to be careful not to say anything to my aunt as she was clearly out of sorts. But with Creepy there, she would only go but so far.

"So let me get this straight," Reesie started when she was abruptly interrupted by my Midnight in shining armor.

"We're not going to do this right now. Matter of fact, how about we don't at all."

Reesie was in no mood to be told what to do with her feelings, but she was in the mood for an explanation from me. How did I get involved with "those people"? How did I so happen to know they would be at my school? Was it all planned? What were her aunts like? Were they really evil like my mother always portrayed them to be? What was my brother like?

"I wish somebody would save me," Reesie confessed while Creepy and I stood in shock. "I wish somebody would save me!"

My aunt plopped herself on the plush, pale pink leather couch that no one sat on, not even on holidays. She put her forehead in the palm of her right hand, her cigarette jutting out from between her middle and pointer fingers, to light the way to a new truth. Reesie was clearly tired of something she never told me, or anyone, about. Not knowing what to do with that moment of vulnerability, I sat on the couch beside her as she pondered God knows what.

"I never had my own life, you know," Reesie began. "Your mother had you, Camille was always away doing her own thing, and I guess she doing good because she never came back or asked for money. Me? I was always Esther's sister, your aunt, somebody's mistress. I lost my momma to some holy rollers, I lost my oldest sister to her own evil, I lost you to God…"

"Reesie," I interrupted. "How can you say you lost me to God?"

"You can't ever come back here living like that. You know how this family feels about that."

"You don't really even know why you feel the way you feel. Mother Tibideau…"

"Mother what? Mother this, mother that, mother mother mother! Ain't no mothers to be spoken of in here. My mother is dead! Your mother is near dead! I'm not a mother, you're not a mother, and for bringing you up in here Creepy is a mother…"

"Nuh uh," Creepy interrupted. "Don't get on a roll and get your bones picked clean in here. No disrespect, but yo! Change the subject. Just change the subject."

"You sound like my sister," Reesie said as she calmed down and began looking for something that either fell between the seat cushions, underneath the pillows, or somewhere on the floor. I grabbed her pack of cigarettes from the floor and tossed it on her lap. She was nervous and it showed because she was still looking for whatever it was the couch must have eaten. She knew better than to sit on that couch.

After a few moments of awkward silence, Reesie asked me to go to my mother's room and get a few items for her to wear in the hospital. She needed her head scarf, slippers for when she finally would get out of the bed, special soap for the nurses to wash her, and other items that would make her comfortable. My mother had never been confined to a hospital bed and wouldn't even visit a hospital even if someone was sick. She said the sickness would follow a person home and wait patiently to attach itself to someone who was holding onto negative emotions or who didn't care about themselves. She said all bad spirits gravitate towards people with low opinions of themselves because when they feel taken over, they will not feel worthy enough to save and therefore not put up a fight; they would just give in.

I shook off my thoughts because I knew my mother's words had the power to haunt me. She was one of those people who would leave a deep impression on someone with the stories she told. She had this gift where even though you didn't believe what she said, it would repeat in your mind like a tape recorder. I prided myself on remembering my mother's advice and the rules of the house like don't sit on the pink couch, don't go in the basement, stay out of certain cabinets, and never go into her bedroom without her permission. For some reason I forgot the last prescription because necessity dictated that I get what I needed for my mother's hospital stay. As I walked down the hall, I felt like I was walking in muck. Each step I took was like bricks were strapped to my feet. The gravity in the house was almost zero and I moved in such slow motion that I saw clouds of dust separate as though they were viscous. *The blood of Jesus. The blood of Jesus. The blood of Jesus.* I kept repeating the phrase in my mind because my mouth could not move. I kept repeating the phrase in my mind because I heard my own heartbeat and it grew so loud that I thought I was holding it in my hand. I kept repeating the phrase in my mind because only the name of Jesus could stop whatever was happening to me.

As I reached for the door and placed my hand on the knob, whatever was on the other side turned it for me. The door flung open and I felt myself begin to choke, except nothing was in my mouth but something was on my neck choking the Jesus out of me. *The blood of Jesus. The blood of Jesus. The blood of Jesus.* I wanted to close my eyes and jump myself out of the experience, but I realized it was not a dream. It was real and something in my mother's room did not want me in there. My eyes refused to look away while death itself paid me a visit.

The thing in the room ran towards me with the speed of a sprinter, her eyes afire, mouth twisted on one side, and hair waving in a false wind. *The blood of Jesus. The blood of Jesus. The blood of Jesus.* As she reached for me, I saw a shield go up in between the two of us, and I heard the sound of iron upon iron as the shield clashed with the chains that were around her hands and feet. At the end of the chain was a tall man holding them, and when he saw the angel that was sent to defend me, his mouth opened wide and I saw fire and souls dancing in the back of his throat. His mouth opened so wide that it began to swallow him, as well as the chains with my mother still attached to them. She began to slide back to be swallowed up by the spirit who held her captive since she was first introduced to my grandmother's magic. I saw the innocent little girl, like the one I remember seeing in Haiti, who wanted someone to save her. *Sauve moi!* She wanted to be saved from a life she did not ask for. She wanted to be saved from a legacy that started with pride and ended in death. Madame Samedie, my mother, Reesie…everybody wanted to be saved yet no one sought to be rescued.

I did my best to turn to the angel to plead with him to save my mother. I silently cried out to Jesus to give her a chance to repent for dealing in the dark. She didn't have a chance because it was my grandmother's fault. She didn't know. She just did what was expected. *Save her Jesus! Save her!* The angel would not let me turn around because I had to see with my own eyes the fate I would suffer if I ever blasphemed against the Holy Ghost and returned to bondage—a bondage that was created for me, but nevertheless was furthered every time I rejected Christ with my superior intelligence.

My mother continued to slide and slide and slide until I saw a sword slam down on the chains and break the links into pieces. The thing that held the chains began to unswallow itself so that it could once again bind my mother up and begin pulling her into the depths of Hell, but the angel would not have it. *The blood of Jesus. The blood of Jesus. The blood of Jesus.* I saw my words float towards my mother and the words turned to blood. They formed a small, red wall the size of a pocket Bible or a large piece of masking tape, and covered her mouth. At the moment the blood touched her mouth, it untwisted and she mouthed four words that I thought I heard but was not sure. I just knew that at the moment she said them, she bowed her knee. I then heard glass shattering all over the house and a pile up of bodies banging on the door of the Doll Room, the Basement, and the Forbidden Cabinets. I got my strength back and it was as though ten men, ten angels, ten everything, jumped inside my body and I flung open every door and every cabinet and began to plead the blood of Jesus Christ and declare that he was Lord, and that everything in the house that was not like God had to go.

As I ran through the house like a mad woman, Creepy had run out the door and Reesie was on the living room floor rocking, crying, and repeating phrases I've heard before in church, "A yo yo yo yo! A yi yi yi yi! A deet deet deet deet!" I left her in God's hands as I grew even bolder and faced the basement door. The righteous indignation in me would not let me be afraid and I marched down those stairs, turned on every light, and pleaded the blood of Jesus all over that place. I laid my hand on every doorpost, every window, every wall, and declared it holy ground. I saw the imps peering at me from dark corners and I marched towards them believing I had a legion of angels behind me. In my mind I saw the Lord's banner, the standard that he raises against my enemies, and rebuked every demonic force in the name of Jesus. By the time I was done, it seemed like the entire basement was a hundred shades lighter, and I remember the sun shot through the window as God's seal of approval. I had won the battle for my mother's spiritual and natural house.

I walked back upstairs to see Reesie still speaking in tongues as the Holy Spirit overshadowed her. He took advantage of her desire to be saved, to be rescued from herself and the life my grandmother imposed upon her. I knelt beside her and did what Mother Tibideau would do. For the first time in my life, I held my aunt in my arms and cried for her, then I began to pray amateur prayers hoping they'd be good enough to be heard. In between rocking and crying with Reesie, I realized what I had done. I had marched around a house full of demons and devils all by myself and entered zones that were forbidden all of my life. I began to become frightened and realized that it had to have been God that made me do it, and apparently he went back to heaven because I felt like a human being again. I scooped Reesie off the floor, grabbed the car keys that Creepy dropped on the floor in his haste to remove himself from the wrath of God, and planned to head for the hospital until I heard the phone ring. It was the hospital. The nurse relayed to me that my mother was conscious but could barely talk. Since she could not speak on the phone, my mother lifted her good hand to her heart and then pointed to the phone.

"She said she loves you," the nurse deciphered. "She is pointing to the Bible and I think she wants me to read something to you...wait a minute...we are in the index section...she's pointing to Philippians...okay, let me see what she's trying to do...no, not the first chapter...the second one...okay...I think she wants me to go down to verse ten...yes, that's the one...it says that at the name of Jesus, every knee should bow, in heaven and on earth and under the earth, and every tongue confess that Jesus Christ is Lord to the glory of God the Father...okay, hold on...okay, now she is pointing to her head and her heart. I think she is trying to tell you that she believes."

I screamed so loud that the house shook with every vibration of my vocal chords. I leaped and cried and ran in circles and cried some more and thanked God a thousand times, forgetting that I had the phone in my hand and that the nurse was on the other end of my screaming. I was so full of energy and zest that I ran outside to be met by Mother Tibideau, my brother, my twin aunts, and the neighbors from across the street that were standing on the lawn holding hands and praying. They had been there the whole time praying for me as I endured the personal battle in my home. Before I could share with Mother Tibideau what had happened, she had this look that she already knew and walked past me to tend to Reesie, who was back on the floor crying and speaking in baby tongues again. Deliverance was taking place in the house.

After Mother Tibideau reacquainted herself with her niece, who she had not seen in years, and introduced Reesie to her nephew, whom she had never seen, everyone piled into two cars to head to the hospital for a family reunion with my mother. On the way Mother Tibideau explained to me what happened in the house and that they were about to ring the bell when the Lord told her to stay outside and pray. She said my battle was a personal one and that I had to know without a shadow of a doubt God was with me. I had to know that the name of Jesus was sufficient, no matter who was or was not around. When I shared with her what happened with my mother, she was far from surprised.

"I knew this day would come. I knew Esther would return," Mother Tibideau said as her voice trailed off. I knew she wished her sister, Augustine, would have had the same fate. "Esther had been trapped inside her body for a long time. She knew if she kept going she would die, especially because she was unsuccessful at grooming you to follow in her footsteps. Esther is no fool. She knows The Way and God had to show himself strong for her to realize she could not avoid him any longer. God is good, yes indeed."

"Have you ever prayed for me?" Reesie asked.

I was surprised at her vulnerability. I had never known my aunt to have a religious bone in her body. Even though she believed in the stuff my mother did, her own involvement was casual. Out of all of her sisters, Reesie was the only one who drifted through life with no particular aim. My mother had her dark dealings and me to focus on and Camille was never around, but I knew she had a career and a life that she enjoyed enough to be absentee.

"Yes, I prayed for you," Mother Tibideau responded. "We prayed for all of you, but especially Suzi. She has a gift like her grandmother and the devil wanted it. He still wants it, but he can't get it! No indeed!"

My great aunt also knew that Reesie wanted to know about the war in the heavenlies between her, the twins, and my grandmother. Instead of overloading her with too much information after so many years of being apart, she thought it best for Reesie to focus on the positive. If she spent too much time trying to figure out the past, she would chip away at the new thing God was trying to do in her heart.

We finally arrived at the hospital to find my mother exhausted yet glowing in a way I had never seen before. When she saw my brother's face, the tears effortlessly flowed from her eyes. She touched his face and hair, and seeing the two of them together made me wonder why I did not recognize my own family's features before the truth came out. The two of them wept while my twin aunts clasped their hands and began praising God as mother and son were reunited. My mother motioned me with her eyes to come to her side and the three of us embraced. Her tears told the story of a mother who was sorry she gave up her son, who lied to his father and said the child was not his in order to keep him in the dark, and guilty about keeping her daughter from all but two other people in her family.

I sensed everyone's agreement that the conversation we should have had so long ago was no longer needed. Asking why and what for would serve no purpose as God had his perfect will occur in all of our lives that day. Revisiting the past would only recreate scenes that did not need to be acted out.

"I think we all should clear the room and let Esther alone with her children," Mother Tibideau said. "We will be out in the waiting room."

My brother pulled up a chair and sat beside my mother so that she would feel more comfortable with him sitting down than towering over her. He took the Bible and began reading about Joseph after his brothers discovered the man they had gone to in order to save them was the brother they betrayed. Michael shared with her how despite all he had been through, Joseph forgave his brothers because it was the plan of God.

"I forgive you. I really do. I had a great life with the mother and father God gave me. I knew about you from when I was a child and Mother Tibideau made sure I understood everything from God's perspective. He saved me from the plans the enemy had for me by using you to abandon me."

I wanted to ask why God deemed him so special that he saved him from the darkness and not me, but he answered my questions before my mind became red enough to ask.

"Suzi, God has a separate plan for everyone. He doesn't love one more than the other. Had you not stayed where you were, there'd be nobody there to dispel the darkness. Your mother is saved today because of what you did in that house. God was already dealing with her, but he used you to bring it to fruition. You're blessed because of it and you will be a great blessing to other women who went through what you did."

My chest swelled with pride as he said those words. I felt a lightness in my body I had never felt before, and I had the feeling that my life had started completely over. My mother had spent her whole life protecting me from that which wound up saving the both of us. I did not feel like I wanted to die, or yell at the moon, or shake my fist at the sky. I was happy and it was hard to believe that moment was real, but it was. And just to make sure, I looked out the window and to my delight, I did not see an angry, crimson sky. Instead it was blue with clouds. Jesus clouds. And it was good.

# 4 EPILOGUE

It had been five years since Charisse's death and the incident that could have killed my mother. I thought about Charisse often as I remembered we both had the same dream of becoming electrical engineers. I graduated college and got the job she probably would have gotten. In her honor, the college awarded Charisse a post-mortem degree since at the time of her death she had enough credits to graduate. Charisse was a smart girl who no one gave any credit. To everyone else she was just a ho on campus, to my mother she was a nuisance, but to me she was my friend. After her death her father was arrested, along with his son Fairisaac, after he turned to the remaining girls in the house to satisfy the lust he had for Charisse.

I had not seen or spoken to Mari since our last phone conversation when I was home to see my mother in the hospital. I heard she had gotten pregnant shortly after she graduated college and decided to get married, at her mother's behest, so as not to embarrass the family. She never went to graduate school or became active in the organizations for which she felt she had to end our friendship. She even decided not to work as her husband made enough money for her to stay home and raise the child. Mari had become her mother, but the way she was unlike her mother was that while Mari was her father' s child, Mari's child was not her husband's. Rumor had it that Naziir finally got to her, but Mari dared not question the paternity of the child lest people would find out she had been unfaithful. The perfect Mari who I knew and loved was a myth and no better than Charisse, and I realized her absence from my life caused me to face a reality from which I once used her false perfection to escape.

After that whole deliverance service that took place in the house that day, Creepy disappeared without a trace. It was almost as though he was a ghost and it was time for him to return the body he borrowed. Mother Tibideau said he was on assignment, that sometimes the devil puts someone in your life to appear as a friend when their only mission is to add a little leaven to your lump. They have just enough good and just enough bad to convince you that they are open and honest about who they are, all the while their influence poisons your bones with the subtlety of the stealthiest alchemist. That would explain why he was the only friend my mother liked because they were birds of a feather.

I did not want to spend too much time thinking of the past as I had a new life that I had been living. I tried not to cry, even though I had a mixture of emotions that day. I had gotten comfortable with crying on command and liked the feeling of freeing my emotions and being vulnerable. I looked in the mirror and realized my mascara was running and that Reesie would flip out if it got on the dress she bought me. I decided to stop trying to cry as I had to get used to change, more change, and change again. As I rose from my chair, I had the familiar feeling of walking through muck with bricks at the bottom of my feet, but this time I was only nervous yet not afraid.

My mother helped me as we both walked slowly down the corridor. I tried not to outpace her as she was still not 100% recovered from her stroke. We walked arm in arm as she kept staring at me in disbelief that we had come so far— so far that my mother no longer had a disdain for holiness white. In fact, she had come to love it like it was her favorite color all along.

We eventually made it to my brother who was at the end of the corridor waiting for us. He was finally a senior pastor at a large church and had the authority to ordain people into ministry. My brother asked my mother a question, to which she gave a reply, then she left me standing up front while she took her seat to watch me say my vows. She and I were both in disbelief that her daughter who was once nearly an atheist, was standing at the altar making a vow to God.

I listened to my brother talk and he asked some questions, to which I replied with the most truth I had ever spoken. He then told me to turn to my right, and as I did, Chuck lifted my veil and kissed his new bride. And I knew from that day forward that the sky would never turn crimson again.

www.ingramcontent.com/pod-product-compliance
Lightning Source LLC
Chambersburg PA
CBHW051952170626
46808CB00007B/2588